Charlie Lister on Greyhounds

Julia Barnes

CHARLIE LISTER'S DEDICATION

I would like to dedicate this book, with thanks, to Dad, Val,
sons Charlie and Richard, daughter Tracey, and all their families.

Published by First Stone,
An imprint of Corpus Publishing Limited
PO Box 8, Lydney,
Gloucestershire, GL15 6YD.

Designed by Sarah Williams.

First Published 2004
Reprinted 2004

ISBN 1 904439 24 1

Printed and bound in Singapore

0 9 8 7 6 5 4 3 2

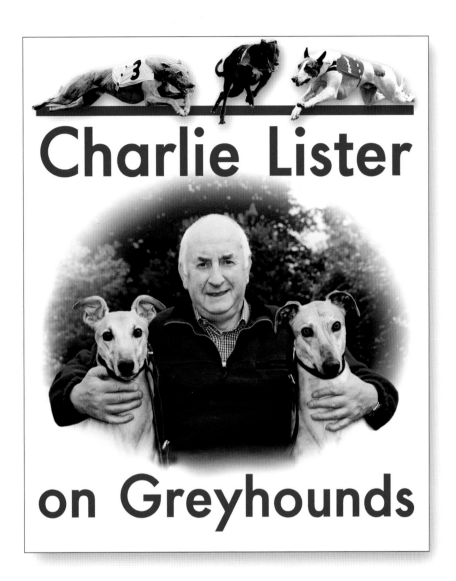

Charlie Lister
on Greyhounds

Julia Barnes

Photography by Steve Nash

FIRST STONE

CONTENTS

FOREWORD

If television was to create a fictional dog trainer, he would surely look a bit like some of the *Greyhound Star*'s old stock photos of Charlie Lister – middle aged, working class, glum, and, of course, sporting a flat cap.

The real Charlie Lister is altogether much more interesting. To begin with, forget the cap. While it might have proved handy to pull over the eyes when trying to get 6-4 in a Chesterfield open, it has long since been binned by Charlie's fashion guru and partner, Pat.

A prop for this former 'King of the Flaps' would probably be an old Vauxhall van.

The real Lister is a successful businessman who brought his first Rolls Royce 30 years ago – not that you would catch him in one these days, at least not until they launch an estate version.

The fictional dog trainer would think nothing about terrorising the local wildlife. Not Charlie.

Like his mentor, the great Joe Booth, Charlie worships all animals. You might see an occasional pet rabbit about the place but it would probably outlive any dozy kennel lad who allowed an open racer to stray within sniffing distance.

Our fictional dog trainer would stop at nothing to turn his runner into a winner. Now Charlie is no pushover. Greyhound folklore has numerous tales of Charlie's prowess in the art of fisticuffs (for obvious reasons, not included in the following pages) but when it comes to his dogs, he is an absolute softie.

To witness Charlie after one of his dogs has been badly injured is to see a man in turmoil. On those rare occasions when the problem is terminal, Charlie is invariably inconsolable. Yes, big tough Charlie!

Even when it is the kindest thing to put an old faithful out of his misery, Pat is summoned to do the deed. Charlie will be off-colour for days.

What other qualities might the reader discover in his quest to find the secret of greyhound training greatness?

Charlie could give masterclasses in 'attention to detail'. How many trainers would put aside half a day just to ensure that he could watch a dog trial – and take a kennel hand so he could watch the trial uninterrupted from the grandstand? (Small wonder, then, if he blows a gasket when a groundsman can't be bothered to take a tractor around or water the first bend correctly.)

Charlie could also have written the authoritative guide to 'Patient Training'. Leaf through the pages and uncover tales of dogs whose recuperation and post-injury preparation ran into seasons rather than months. Eager owners were forced to sit out a string of lucrative competitions until Charlie was satisfied that the healing process was complete.

However, having studied many of the finest handlers ever to have held a greyhound on a lead, I reckon the greatest attribute is one that cannot easily be defined or explained – a God-given gift.

It goes beyond knowledge, observation and experience. It is the ability to understand a dog at a very rare level.

Former champion trainer Linda Mullins, one of the sport's least dotty characters, once told me that she truly believed that her dogs 'ran for her'. I believe it. That affinity between hound and handler distinguishes great trainers from good ones.

This book is not about a good greyhound trainer. In our often maligned and undervalued sport, Charlie Lister is, quite simply, a living legend.

Floyd Amphlett
Editor, *Greyhound Star*.

CHAPTER ONE

GRASS ROOTS

To some, greyhound racing may be a hobby. To others, it is a job. To Charlie Lister, it is, quite simply, an obsession. Charlie lives and breathes greyhounds in a way that means everything, and everyone, else comes a poor second. He has been involved in greyhound racing for most of his life, and, although he is now in his early sixties, he is as passionate about the subject as ever.

"I love to see my greyhounds run. I cannot rest if I know my dogs are racing. Of course, I love to win. It doesn't matter how many big competitions I have won, there is still no bigger thrill for me than watching one of my dogs cross the winning line."

If he isn't at the track watching his greyhounds run, there is always racing on Sky TV, which his long-time partner, Pat Cartledge, records for him to watch if he has to have an evening in. Failing that, there are always videos of his greyhounds' greatest victories...

Pat is happily resigned to Charlie's passion for greyhound racing. When they first started going out, he asked her where she wanted to go. "The Peak District," she replied.

"I hope that's near Peterborough," said Charlie, "I've got a dog running there tonight."

"If Charlie is at home for a couple of nights and doesn't go racing, he gets really restless," said Pat. "He's itching to get back to the track."

That intense dedication has certainly paid off, for Charlie is unquestionably the top greyhound trainer in the Britain. His small open race kennel has produced star after star, and there are few major competitions he has failed to win. His outstanding achievements include winning the Greyhound Derby four times (twice with the same dog – Rapid Ranger – in 2000 and 2001), winning the Scottish and English Derby in the same year (1997) with Some Picture, who also went on to reach the final of the Irish Classic, and pulling off a classic double when Spring Rose triumphed in the Grand Prix and the St. Leger in 1996.

Charlie has a gift for finding the right dog for the right competition, and, in some cases, such as the East Anglian Derby at Yarmouth, it takes a brave trainer to challenge him. He has won the competition a record seven times!

At the end of 2003 Charlie reached another notable milestone. He won the Trainers' Championship for the first time, obtaining a record number of points – a remarkable achievement for a trainer with no more than 30 greyhounds, competing against trainers with up to 200 dogs in their charge.

"I've never intentionally gone out to be a champion trainer. We just won a few finals, worked extremely hard, and had a bit of luck – but we never really pushed it," said Charlie.

EARLY DAYS

Charlie Lister is a Yorkshireman by birth, although Nottinghamshire has become very much his adopted home. He was born in 1940, and was brought up in the small village of Rawcliffe, near Goole, in the East Riding. His father, Charles, made a living out of buying and selling horses.

"I was brought up rough and ready. My father made a living, but there was never much money around. He made a bit, but he liked spending it too!"

Charlie was an only child, and he spent much of his childhood with his father, going to horse fairs and watching his father at work.

"In those days, horses were used for farm work and as carthorses, and so the fairs were busy places. I went to Doncaster Fair every Saturday, and it was a great place to be."

Charlie watched his father trotting horses up, assessing their value, and it was there that he first developed an eye for an animal.

"You can learn a lot just by looking at an animal and watching the way it moves. We were on the look out for splints and spavins – anything that might affect the horse when he was working."

Charlie was brought up in a small cottage, with a couple of stables in the backyard. There were always dogs in the family, but they were not pets. They were coursing dogs.

"I was seven or eight when I started going coursing with my father. We had greyhound crosses – probably three-parts greyhound. Right from the start, I loved watching the dogs run. My dad was good with the dogs, and, over the years, I learned a lot from him. He understood about feeding them and keeping them happy."

Among his childhood friends was Geoff de Mulder, the trainer of 1979 English Derby winner Sarahs Bunny, and a host of other top greyhounds.

"We saw a lot of each other when we were kids. His father was in the meat trade, and, like my dad, he also dealt in horses. We have always got on well – he's a great character."

BRANCHING OUT

Charlie left school when he was 12, and from that day onwards, he has had to earn his own living.

"My mum and dad didn't mind me leaving school. I was more use bringing some money into the family than staying at school."

Charlie's first job was selling flowers at the local market, and he picked up a bit of extra cash betting on his coursing dogs. When he was 15, the family moved to Worksop, in Nottinghamshire, and it was there he was approached by a young entrepreneur who was looking for a partner to buy a load of timber.

"The deal was that I put up the money, and we shared the profit. I decided to give it a go, and we made a bit of money selling off the timber. We carried on working together for the next 12 months or so, buying up timber and then selling it, and then I decided to set up on my own.

"I was always good at figures, and I understood about making a profit. If I bought a load of timber for £50, I sold it for £100 – it was as simple as that."

The business started to take off, and Charlie acquired a lorry. "I set off on a Monday with a full load of timber, and went round the local farms selling it. Sometimes I would be back home with an empty lorry by Tuesday, other times it took longer. But I was in a good area. There were lots of farms, and timber was needed for building and for fencing. I soon built up a round of regular customers."

Charlie is the first to admit that he didn't know anything about timber, and very little about business in those early days. "I had no knowledge; I just picked it

Building up the timber business took up most of Charlie's time, but he was becoming increasingly involved with greyhound racing.

up as I went along. I think you just develop an eye for looking at things, and being able to judge their value."

He was always lightning fast to spot a business opportunity. "I got a yard at East Markham in Nottinghamshire, and there was a dispute with the council because it was restricted to agricultural use. I managed to get planning permission for five houses on the site before I sold it, so I managed to make a few quid out of that."

The business flourished, and, before long, Charlie had a fleet of 10 lorries working out of his yard. He was just 18 when he married his first wife, and soon they had a young family. "The family and

the business took up most of my time, but I always kept an interest in coursing. In those days you could pick up a decent coursing dog for between £10 and £20. It was a hobby for me, although I made a bit on the coursing matches we ran. But as the timber business grew, I had less time for the dogs."

ON TRACK

Charlie might have spent the rest of life as a coursing man had it not been for a routine health check. "I was applying for my heavy goods vehicle licence, and I had to have a health check. I don't think I had ever been to a doctor before. Anyway, he found out that I had high blood pressure, and he said I should take more exercise.

"There was a lad working for me and he was keen on flapping, and he asked me to go to a track with him. I wasn't that keen, as I thought coursing was the better sport, but I agreed to go along. When I got there, I surprised myself because I really enjoyed it. I thought that if I got a greyhound and kept it at home, it would make me take more exercise."

Charlie bought his first racing greyhound – and from that day onwards he became a convert to track racing. "To be honest, that first greyhound wasn't very good, but I started learning. I got some more dogs and I began winning a few races. People could see that I knew what I was doing, and I started to take on dogs for other people."

Charlie's first marriage ended in divorce, but in 1968 he married Val, who soon became absorbed in the world of greyhound racing.

KING OF THE FLAPS

It was at this point that Charlie met the legendary greyhound trainer Joe Booth. Joe was a highly successful NGRC trainer, and as Charlie did not have a trainer's licence at the time, he put a couple of his best dogs with Joe. Joe's greyhounds were well known on the NGRC circuit, but they also lived another life, running incognito on flapping tracks.

Joe toured the country, placing his dogs in races and pulling off major betting coups. Unsubstantiated rumours put his record in the Ashfield Derby at six, the Wishaw Spring Cup at the same number, the Peterborough Derby at eight, the Ipswich Derby at six (three times on the bounce), and the Yarmouth Derby at six – possibly more.

"Of course, you were not allowed to run NGRC dogs at flapping tracks, but it happened all the time. Whenever my dogs were racing, I travelled with Joe, and I learnt a lot from him.

"He was a brilliant man with dogs. He was very kind to them, and he fed them well. He had a knack of getting dogs to produce their best. If a dog was a bit jaded, he would take him for a walk in the woods so that the dog could see rabbits and squirrels. It was just enough to sharpen up a dog."

Joe Booth is remembered for his spectacular betting coups, but he also pulled off some amazing feats of training.

"The dog I remember is Cricket Bunny. When Joe bought him, he was a graded racer at Wimbledon, and he wasn't really chasing. Joe took him away, and bought him back to win the Laurels in 1972 – it was the biggest race at Wimbledon at that time.

"Joe was good at placing dogs in the right races, and I learnt a lot from him on that score. He trained dogs for 50 years, and made a good living out of them. He was known at every track in the country, and every trainer admired him.

"He was never attached to a track, he just made a living out of the dogs in his care. In all the time I knew him, he never had more than 10 dogs at a time. Believe me, you have got to be very clever to make a living with that number of dogs."

Joe Booth straddled the NGRC/flapping world like a giant colossus, keeping a foot firmly in each camp – but not falling foul of the NGRC. How did he do it?

"The great thing about Joe was that he kept everything to himself. He didn't tell anyone more than they needed to know. In fact, it was always said of him that his left hand didn't know what his right hand was doing."

THE INDEPENDENT CIRCUIT

Charlie was now winning big races in his own right, and, in his time as a flapping man, he won most of the major

competitions on the independent circuit. He won the Ashfield Derby twice and the Blackpool Derby three times. But, in the end, he became frustrated by the restrictions that were forced upon him.

"The dogs were my hobby, but it's nice to have a hobby that pays. I liked having a bet, but I liked watching my dogs run even more. When I became well known on the circuit, I couldn't take a dog into the track because I wouldn't get a price. You had to hire men, known as jockeys, who would take the dogs in for you while you waited in the car park, or a few streets away.

"There was one time at Bury St. Edmunds when I got a local team to take a dog in for me. I said I would come in as soon as they had put the money on. The next thing I knew someone was thumping on the car window. I had fallen asleep while my dog had romped home!"

In the end, it was the frustration of having to be incognito on race nights that led to Charlie's decision to become an NGRC trainer.

"If you've got a good dog, you want to see him run. It got more and more difficult for me to do that, and I thought: 'What's the point?' It was great to pull off the coups, but I was missing out on the most important part."

CHAPTER TWO

UNDER RULES

Charlie took out an NGRC permit licence in the early 1970s, and started to build his reputation as a trainer under rules. He soon switched to an owner-trainer licence so that he could become involved in the open race circuit. It was not long before he was pulling off open race raids at the permit tracks – and this gave him a taste for the big time.

"I started to get some good dogs, and I was confident that I could compete at some of the bigger tracks. The first top-class greyhound I had when I was racing NGRC was Superior Champ. He was a very good dog, and I won a lot of races with him.

"We travelled up and down the country competing at different tracks. His best wins were the Silver Salver at Southend in 1978, and the Northern Sprint at Sheffield in 1980."

He also won the Manchester Puppy Cup at Belle Vue with Meanus Duke in 1979. From this period on, Charlie's allegiance has been firmly with the NGRC, but he still remains loyal to his independent roots.

"You hear a lot of bad things said about flapping, but most of them are not true. People think it is all about stopping dogs, but they are wrong.

"In my experience, most of the tracks are well run, and some are definitely superior to NGRC circuits. The flapping people know their dogs and they treat them well. When a dog has finished racing, he will often be kept on as a pet. That is not nearly so often the case with NGRC owners."

Charlie had some good dogs, but,

Success as a track trainer. Pictured (left to right): Ray Andrews (Leeds), Harry Crapper (Sheffield), and Charlie, then attached to Nottingham.

initially he found it harder to win races on the NGRC tracks. "When you are flapping, there are probably two outstanding dogs in the race, and the others are fairly average. When you are racing under rules, the standard is more consistent; often you are up against five other dogs who all have a reasonable chance of winning."

TRACK TRAINER

Charlie has been attached to a number of NGRC tracks, including Nottingham, Sheffield, Peterborough, Leicester and Leeds. But he greatly prefers the freedom of being able to operate independently.

"I have a good relationship with the tracks where I have been attached, but, for me, graded racing is not enough of a challenge. I could never really take to it. I don't like going to the same track week in week out, and watching the same dogs racing against each other.

"Once you have got a good dog into the top two or three grades, it then becomes a matter for the racing office to decide how a race is going to be run. You are entirely in their hands. I understand that they must give dogs a reasonable chance, but I like to go out knowing that I can win.

"I started off racing on the independent circuit and going after the big races, and I suppose graded racing never really measured up to that."

OPEN RACERS

Charlie had some decent open racers throughout the eighties. He won the first of his string of East Anglian Derbies at Yarmouth in 1981 with Swift Band (Yellow Band - Swift Lass), who crossed the line in a time of 28.33 for the 462m trip. In the same year, Fox Fire won the Mackworth Dash at Derby. Yellow

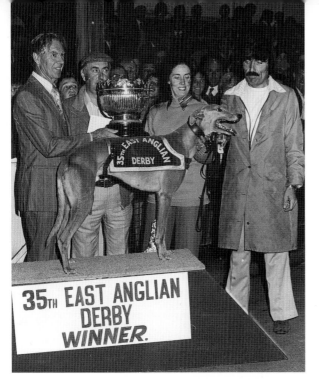

Swift Band: Winner of the 1981 East Anglian Derby. It was the first of many big wins at the seaside track for Charlie (second left).

Cowboy (Yellow Ese – Lenas Blackie) won a big invitation stakes at Crayford in 1982, Spots Of Condor (Lindas Champion – Spots of Sanyo) won the Puppy Cup at Belle Vue in 1983, and Night Runner (Knockrour Slave – Hi There Linda) won the Northern Sprint Championship at Sheffield in 1986. The following year Bleakhall Wonder won the Derby Plate, and Jers Pick took the Pepsi Cola Sprint at Yarmouth.

Yarmouth has always been a lucky track for Charlie, and in 1990 Artie Joe won a second East Anglian Derby for him. The son of I'm Slippy recorded a winning time of 28.57. Slideaway Snoopy (Michigan

Man – Marys Mascot) shared the honours that year, winning the Sunderland Oaks and the Peterborough Cesarewitch. A hat-trick of Northern Sprint wins was completed when Bank Tunnel (Dads Bank – Tunnel Man) took the event in 1992, and top open race wins were recorded by Risk It Miss (The Other Risk – Wish Miss) in the Diamond Jubilee 500 at Sheffield, and the Milligans Bakery Challenge at Sunderland.

It was from the early nineties that the kennel really took off. "I had a lot of owners ringing me up, asking if I would take their greyhounds. I decided that it was time to hand over the timber business to my two sons and go into training full-time. Val and I moved to the new house at South Clifton, and the greyhounds came with us. I can honestly say that I have never looked back."

STAR SIX

Charlie's life-changing decision was marked with almost instant success, and he remembers 1993 as being a dream year for his Mudros kennel.

"We had six outstanding greyhounds. We got to the finals of most of the major competitions – and then we won our fair share."

The six dogs were: Callahow Daly (Daleys Gold – Ahaveen Fever), Droopys Slave (Manorville Magic – Twilight Slave), Justright Kyle (Kyle Jack – I'm A Duchess), Killeenagh Dream (Dads Bank – Killenagh Lady), Simply Free (Daleys Gold – Rooskey Critic), and Sure Fantasy (Phantom Flash – Lively Spark II).

In one glorious year, Callahow Daly won the Harry Holmes Memorial at Sheffield (he went on to give Charlie his first Greyhound Derby finalist the following year), and Droopys Slave won the Gold Cup at Brough Park (a triumph he repeated the following year). Justright Kyle had a remarkable run, taking the Archie Scott Memorial and the Midland Flat, both at Hall Green, plus the East Anglian Derby at Yarmouth in a time of 28.30.

"Justright Kyle started his career racing up north when Tommy Robinson was training him. I saw him run at Nottingham. He won, but in a slow time. I was still impressed with him – I liked his action. I wasn't that worried about the time; I thought the track was running slow. In my own mind, I knew he was a

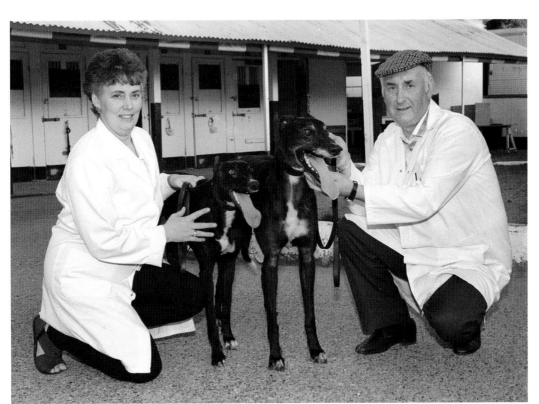

Big winners in 1993: Justright Kyle and Simply Free pictured with Val and Charlie.

lot faster. I said to Tommy that I would buy the dog if he ever wanted to sell. He wasn't interested, and Just Right Kyle went on to win quite a few races, but then he went off the boil and wasn't running so well.

"Tommy rang me to see if I was still interested, but I said: 'Why should I be? The dog isn't running well.' Anyway, I agreed to take the dog if he was sound, and one of my owners, Frank Kearney, agreed to buy him. I decided to give the dog a month off, and to start afresh with him. He had been down as a wide runner, but I thought he looked more of a railer. I changed him over, and then everything seemed to click."

Sure Fantasy won the Peterborough Puppy Derby, followed by the November Grand and the Xmas Cup at Sheffield, and Simply Free took honours in the Midland Oaks at Hall Green, the Yorkshire Oaks at Sheffield, and the prestigious Select Stakes at Wembley, winning in a time of 29.16. Killeenagh Dream was the first marathon dog for the kennel, winning the Key at Wimbledon, and notching the Cesarewitch at Belle Vue in a time of 55.21 for the 853m trip.

"I first saw Killeenagh Dream running graded at Belle Vue. He had been bought cheaply, and even though he had a good Irish card, he wasn't doing anything. The owners couldn't understand what was going wrong, and so they asked me if I would take the dog. I said I would take him for a month, and see how he got on.

"I looked at the dog running, and I thought: 'He looks a bit one-paced –

Killeenagh Dream: Winner of the 1993 Cesarewitch. He was Charlie's first top-class marathon dog.

maybe he's more of a stayer.' At this point, he had only been raced over four bends.

"We tried him over six bends and he immediately started to improve. He started winning open races, and then we decided to try him in the Cesarewitch. We had the great satisfaction of taking him back to Belle Vue and seeing him win the competition in fine style. He also came second in the TV Trophy."

There were other greyhounds that also boosted the kennel's winning tally, such as Spenwood Magic (Westmead Claim – Loopy Lil), who won the William King Cup at Shawfield and the Dransfield St. Leger at Sheffield, and Monard Wish (Whisper Wishes – Solas An Maiden), winner of the Cock O' The North at Belle Vue.

Charlie's kennel was the talk of the greyhound racing world, and he seemed to be unstoppable, but then tragedy struck. In 1994 he lost his wife, Val, to cancer. "It was a terrible blow. She was only 47. She was diagnosed with cancer, and then she was clear for two years. But she was in a minor car accident, and it triggered the return of the disease. I took it very hard and I was depressed for a long time afterwards."

It was a couple of years later that the kennel lads took Charlie out for a drink to the local pub to try to cheer him up. There he met Pat Cartledge, who already had an interest in greyhounds. She had a dog that she took flapping at Chesterfield. That was the start of a new era, and since then Pat has been Charlie's partner, as well as being a highly valued member of the team at Mudros.

STAYING POWER

Following Val's death, 1994 was a comparatively quiet year for the Mudros kennel. Sure Fantasy continued his winning ways when he took the Archie Scott Benevolent Trophy at Hall Green, and Sunhill Misty (Kyle Jack – Game Misty) made her mark over the marathon distance, winning a feature event over 820m at Walthamstow – the Pepsi Cola Marathon – in 53.19, and the Daily Record Marathon at Shawfield. Chadwell Charmer (Fly Cruiser – Slippery Moth) showed good form in winning two major puppy events at Sunderland and at Brough Park, and Tammys Delight (Waltham Abbey – Lulus Moth) won the Dransfield Novelty Ebor at Sheffield.

The kennel was back making headlines in 1995 when Dragon Prince, a son of Whisper Wishes, took a liking to

Dragon Prince: Winner of the 1995 East Anglian Derby – the fourth victory for Charlie in this event.

Yarmouth and won the East Anglian Challenge and the East Anglian Derby. His winning time was 28.56.

Glamour Hobo (Nameless Star – Glamour Show) won the Bedfordshire Derby at Henlow, Harrys Boy Blue (Tico – Soviet Supreme) won the Dean Jackson Memorial at Hull, Tailors Noel (Balinderry Ash – Tailors Rush) took the Northern Sprint at Sheffield, and the black bitch Dinan Wonder (Druids Johno – Cavecourt Bet) was first in the Midland St. Leger at Monmore. Egmont Joan (Daleys Gold – Egmont Biddy) showed the bitches the way home in the Northern Oaks at Belle Vue.

Charlie's reputation for picking dogs to win races was already well established, and the prolific winner Suncrest Sail (Low Sail – Sarahs Surprise) was a terrific example of his ability to keep a dog in top form for long periods. Racing over two seasons, he proved virtually unbeatable over six and eight bends. His 1995 wins included the NGRC Stewards Cup at Walthamstow, the Regency at Hove, the Dransfield Novelty Ebor at Sheffield, the Regal St. Leger at Shawfield, capping it with the Grand Prix at Walthamstow, which he won in 39.62 for the 640m. The following year, his victories included the Dransfield Ebor at Sheffield, the William King Cup at Shawfield, and the TV Trophy at Walthamstow, which he won in 51.75 for the 820m course.

"Suncrest Sail was with Geoff de Mulder before he came to me. The owners had a

fall out with Geoff and asked me if I would take the dog over. Geoff is a friend, and I said I wouldn't do anything until I had talked to Geoff. He said: 'If you don't take him, he'll only go to someone else', so I agreed.

"At this point he hadn't done very much. He had won a couple of races but he had an injury problem. The first time I trialled him was at Sheffield. The owners wanted to know what I thought of him, and I had to say: 'Not a lot.' I examined him, and found he had a problem with his shoulder. We treated it, and, after a couple more trials, he came to himself, and he couldn't stop winning.

"He got on a winning reel, and he notched up 15 races on the trot. I could have kept building up a sequence if I had picked one-off races, but I was more interested in going for the big competitions. I had him at a time when I only kept 10-15 dogs, and so he really did win a lot of races for me.

Spring Rose: Winner of the 1996 Grand Prix and St. Leger. She goes down as one of Charlie's all-time great greyhounds.

"He was a good dog over six bends and over eight bends. He had tremendous middle pace. He could come from behind, and he was never really beat. He would come off a bend and pick dogs up. He was pretty consistent out of the boxes, but if he missed his break, he could make up the ground."

SPRING ROSE

Another significant development for the kennel was the emergence of a white and fawn bitch called Spring Rose (Galtymore Lad – Rachels Baby), a greyhound Charlie rates as one of his all-time greats. In an amazing run, she went unbeaten through the 1996 Grand Prix at Walthamstow, and, in the same year, she won the St. Leger at Wembley. She was British Greyhound of the Year in 1996, and she has been given a place in the Greyhound Hall of Fame.

"She was lovely to look at – a good-size bitch of around 66-67 pounds. She had early pace, and she could stay forever.

"I started running her over middle distances and she recorded some good times. She reached the final of the Puppy Classic at Nottingham and finished in second place.

"She had the early pace to lead, but she ran on so strongly that I decided to keep her to six bends. She was one of the best staying bitches I have ever trained. On her day she was absolutely brilliant. I think she would have stayed 800m, but she got injured, so I wasn't able to try her. She was always very nervous, but she loved her racing.

"We mated her, but there was only three pups in the litter and one died. We mated her again, and from two pups she produced TV Trophy winner Sexy Delight. In her last litter she had only one pup, so we didn't mate her again. She is still living with us in the kennel."

*Some Picture:
Charlie was
quick to see
his potential.*

SOME PICTURE

Charlie was now rated all round as an outstanding handler of top-class greyhounds, but the big breakthrough came in October 1996 when a black dog by the name of Some Picture (Slaneyside Hare – Spring Season) arrived in the kennel.

Charlie said: "He was brought over from Ireland in October 1996 after winning the Dunmore Puppy Cup. He then went flapping with Alf Pennycock. He raced in Scotland and the north of England, and soon got a reputation for his pace. He was breaking track records everywhere. Out of the blue, Alf rang up and asked me if I would run the dog for him. He was a good judge of a greyhound, so I agreed, and I entered him in the Eclipse Stakes at Nottingham. He won his heat and was ante-post favourite to win the final.

"Alf rang up and said, if he was offered £11,000, he would sell. I immediately rang up Steve Spiteri, owner of Spring Rose, to see if he wanted the dog. He said: 'How good a dog is he?', and I said: 'Very good.' He asked me to buy the dog for him. It was a good day's work, as Some Picture went on to win the Eclipse Stakes at Nottingham, the Select Stakes at Wembley, the Scottish Derby and the English Derby.

"He was a big, fine-looking dog when he arrived in the kennel, and I liked everything about him. He was the sort of dog who stood out and said, 'Look at me.' He was confident and self-assured. He was clean in his kennel and no trouble to

FACT FILE

Spring Rose takes honours in the 1996 Grand Prix. Pictured (left to right) Sarah, Stephanie and Paul Spiteri, their father, Steve, Charlie, and Michael Harris.

Spring Rose
- w f bitch
- January 1994
- Born: Ireland
- Breeder: Rachel Dolan
- Owner: Steve Spiteri

Galtymore Lad

Moral Support

Yellow Band

Melody La Moore

Borris Chat

Daring Dandy

Virginia Chat

Rachels Baby

Im Slippy

Laurdella Fun

Glenroe Bess

Dennys Daisy

Sand Man

Lindas Zest

Spring Rose started her career racing over four bends, and reached the final of the Puppy Classic at Nottingham in 1995 when she was runner-up to Elliots Gem. Her six-bend debut was delayed through injury, but then she quickly proved that staying was her game. She competed over Wembley's 655m course and stormed home by 10 lengths.

The Grand Prix at Walthamstow was her next test, and the white and fawn bitch looked in a class of her own as she broke the track record twice during the 640m competition, winning the final in 39.05 by eight lengths.

As always, Charlie had her racing campaign mapped out, and her next test was the St. Leger at Wembley. Again, Spring Rose went unbeaten through the competition, and stormed home in the final, clocking a track record of 39.29 for the 655m, and beating Wise Beauty by almost eight lengths. She was only the second greyhound in racing history to complete the Grand Prix/St. Leger double, following on from Huberts Shade's remarkable achievement in 1982. It was enough to make her Greyhound of the Year in 1996.

Charlie had the Grand Prix and St. Leger in mind again the following year, and apart from a record-breaking run at Monmore, she was confined to trials in the build-up to the 1997 big races. She looked back to her best when she ran unbeaten to reach the Grand Prix final, but this time she was pipped at the post by El Grand Senor.

She looked on course for the 1997 St. Leger, and she was made 2/1 on favourite for the final, but she was injured during the race, and finished fifth.

This marked the end of her racing career, but her legacy lived on in Sexy Delight. This bitch was the result of a mating with 1997 Scottish and English Derby winner Some Picture. Bred in the purple, she was a prolific open race winner and went on to collect the TV Trophy in 2000.

Spring Rose in the semi-finals of the 1996 St. Leger. She won by four lengths from One For Tarbert.

Derby triumph: Charlie and connections after Some Picture wins the 1997 Greyhound Derby in style.

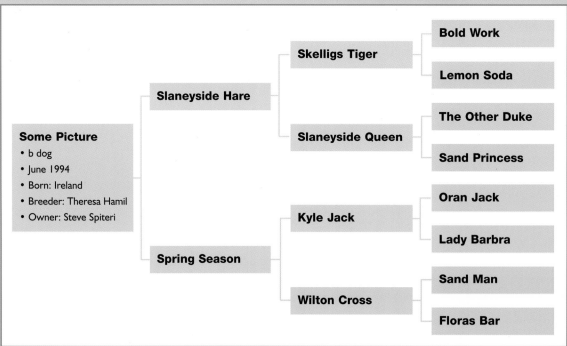

Some Picture
- b dog
- June 1994
- Born: Ireland
- Breeder: Theresa Hamil
- Owner: Steve Spiteri

Slaneyside Hare

Spring Season

Skelligs Tiger

Slaneyside Queen

Kyle Jack

Wilton Cross

Bold Work

Lemon Soda

The Other Duke

Sand Princess

Oran Jack

Lady Barbra

Sand Man

Floras Bar

There was no other greyhound worth talking about in the year 1997. The black, Irish-bred dog won the Scottish and English Derbies back to back, and came very close to adding the Irish Derby to his winning score.

Some Picture first grabbed the headlines when he won the Eclipse at Nottingham in 1996, where his fine running style and electric pace gave rise to comment. He started favourite for the final and crossed the line in 29.83 for the 500m course. He was invited to compete in the Select Stakes at Wembley, and was an easy winner in 28.91 for the 490m.

In 1997, Charlie Lister aimed Some Picture at the Regal Scottish Derby, and the son of Slaneyside Hare was untroubled by the opposition. He reached the final unbeaten, and then clocked a fast 28.20 to win the decider from trap five, two lengths clear of Elderberry Chick. This was some achievement, and connections were quick to note that Regal were offering a £100,000 bonus to any greyhound that won the Scottish Derby, and then went on to win the English and Irish equivalents.

Some Picture proved he was in a class of his own with a spectacular, unbeaten run through the English Derby. In the final, he was the unsurprising 8-13 favourite to take the £50,000 prize, and he did not give supporters a moment's worry. Drawn in trap six, he was ahead by the second bend and romped home to beat He Knows by 6¼ lengths in a brilliant 28.23, the fastest time recorded in a Derby at Wimbledon.

The Irish Derby – and the £100,000 bonus – now seemed like a realisable dream. Everything went according to plan for the first two rounds – but then illness struck, and Charlie had to nurse his star through to the final. He was beaten into fifth place behind Toms The Best, but in the circumstances it was a remarkable feat to get that far. Some Picture goes down in greyhound racing history as one of the all-time greats, and, on his retirement, he was elected to the Hall of Fame.

Continued on page 28

Some Picture (6) on his way to victory in the 1997 Greyhound Derby final. Stows Val (3) and Annies Bullet (5) dispute an early lead on the inside. They are followed by Heres Andy (2) and eventual runner-up He Knows (4).

SOME PICTURE: DERBY FINAL RESULTS

1997 REGAL SCOTTISH DERBY: FINAL RESULT

Fin.	Name	Sex	Sire	Dam	Time	Dist.	Box	Sp.
1st	Some Picture	M	Slaneyside Hare	Spring Season	29.20		5	evens f
2nd	Elderberry Chick	F	Adraville Bridge	Mindys Miracle	29.36	2	3	4-1
3rd	Endon Tiger	M	Slaneyside Hare	Kevalnig Kwik	29.37	nk	4	4-1
4th	Quick Tune	M	Farloe Melody	Lady Be Fast	29.49	1½	6	8-1
5th	Airmount Jeff	M	Airmount Spec	Airmount Mary	29.57	1	2	3-1
6th	Donnas Dancer	F	Kildare Asj	Greenwood Beauty	29.61	½	1	25-1

1997 ENGLISH DERBY: FINAL RESULT

Fin.	Name	Sex	Sire	Dam	Time	Dist.	Box	Sp.
1st	Some Picture	M	Slaneyside Hare	Spring Season	28.23		6	8-13f
2nd	He Knows	M	Slaneyside Hare	I Know You	28.73	6¼	4	3-1
3rd	Stows Val	F	Polnoon Chief	Polnoon Lane	28.77	½	3	10-1
4th	Annies Bullet	F	Slippys Quest	O Hickey Kylie	29.07	3¾	5	7-1
5th	Charpaidon	M	Cravencottage UK	Kildare Raven	29.09	¼	1	33-1
6th	Heres Andy	M	Polnoon Chief	Minnies Nikita	29.33	3	2	7-1

1997 IRISH DERBY: FINAL RESULT

Fin.	Name	Sex	Sire	Dam	Time	Dist.	Box	Sp.
1st	Toms The Best	M	Frightful Flash	Ladys Guest	30.09		6	4-1
2nd	Vintage Prince	M	Slaneyside Hare	Ferbane Skippy	30.14	¾	3	9-4
3rd	Right To Apply	M	Frightful Flash	Hymenstown Lynn	30.30	2¼	2	16-1
4th	Jokers Run	M	Deenside Joker	Dream Run	30.56	3¾	1	25-1
5th	Some Picture	M	Slaneyside Hare	Spring Season	30.58	hd	5	9-4
6th	Spiral Nikita	M	Phantom Flash	Minnies Nikita	30.62	½	4	3-1

handle. Nothing fazed him.

"I gave him a couple of trials at Nottingham, and I knew I had a good dog. He was a wide runner, but he was very brainy. He went into a bend, and then cut in. But if there were dogs on the inside, he kept on the outside. He could run the bends as fast as the straights. He could go into a bend a couple of lengths behind and come out in front. He was literally coursing the hare.

"He was a good trapper, but he could also come from behind. We didn't try him over six bends, although he looked as if he could stay – he was so powerful, and he was terrifically well balanced. He was a very determined runner.

"His first major event was the 1997 Scottish Derby. He won all four rounds, and in the final he clocked the fastest time in the competition.

"Obviously we had the English Derby in mind. I was not sure how well he would run Wimbledon, as there is a long run to the first bend, but he had no problems. He even took the noise of the Derby roar in his stride. He couldn't possibly hear the sound of the hare, but he trapped with the rise of the lids."

After winning the Scottish Derby and the English Derby, Some Picture was on a bonus of £100,00 if he could pull off the treble and win the Irish Derby. Charlie is not keen to stay away from home, but he thought it was in the dog's best interests to give him a settled spell in Ireland while he was competing. He took him to Michael Dunphy's kennel, and both he and the dog stayed there for the duration of the competition. Some Picture began in good form, but then his luck ran out.

"He was not running his best, and then he started vomiting. I wanted to withdraw him, but there was so much money involved that it was a big problem. In the final, he ran flat.

"We decided to retire him after the final. Steve wanted him to stand at stud in England, but I thought he would be better off in Ireland. I knew he would get better quality bitches, and it would get his stud

career off to a good start. It was decided that he should stay with Michael Dunphy in Ireland. That meant I had to travel back without him. It was one of the hardest things I have ever done. I couldn't speak to anyone; I just left the kennel and made for the car."

Some Picture was very promising at stud, but tragically he died from a heart attack only 18 months after retiring from the track.

"Even in that short time he threw some decent dogs – sprinters, stayers and middle distance. I reckon that, if he had lived, he could have been really influential.

"For me, there was something really special about Some Picture. He was always bold, which I think is a good thing in a racing dog. If you gave him a bone, and he didn't want to give it up, you would go back later and take it when he was ready. He was not a dog to mess with. He always gave the impression that he knew he was a top dog, and that he should be treated like one."

REAPING REWARDS

An open race kennel must have top-class greyhounds, and they don't come cheap. That means a trainer must gain the confidence of owners who have money to

Terrydrum Kate: A storming finish to the 1997 East Anglian Derby.

spend on acquiring the very best. Charlie has never been short of owners wanting to place their dogs with him, and many have stayed with him since his early days as a trainer.

"I built up a good reputation on the independent circuit of winning a lot of big races. Some of the owners have stayed with me from the earliest times. Frank Kearney, Tom Wardle and Bert Ullyett have all had dogs with me for over 25 years. Once I got my NGRC licence and started to win some decent races, I got enquiries from more owners. Steve Spiteri has been with me a long and I trained for professional gambler Harry Findlay before he got his own licence.

"I trained a lot of good dogs before Some Picture came along. Superior Champ and Swift Band were top class, but winning the Derby gave my reputation a boost. A lot of owners who have money to spend live in the south, and they like to have their dogs trained near London. But after the Derby win, when my name became better known, there were more owners who wanted me to have their dogs – even though I was based some distance away.

"Ray White had a good few dogs in

London. He spent a lot of money on his greyhounds and he sent them to a number of different trainers. Then, one day, he asked me if I wanted to take on his dogs. I agreed, but only if I was allowed to sort out which dogs were worth keeping.

"Ever since then I have trained his dogs, and we have had some top-class greyhounds, including Rapid Ranger (Greyhound Derby winner 2000 and 2001). Ray doesn't interfere, and he's become a good friend over the years.

"I have proved that I can train dogs, and there is never a shortage of people who want to put their dogs with me."

Charlie's first Greyhound Derby win was the crowning glory on a memorable year when his kennel continued to dominate the top events. Ballyard Recruit (Deenside Park – Bower Sinead) won the Racing Post Puppy Cup at Romford, beating Greenfield Angel by 1½ lengths in a time of 24.19 for the 400m trip, and Brannigan's Gig (Just Right Kyle – Castelyons Link) took honours in the Northern Flat at Belle Vue, winning the 460m event in 28.00. Cry Havoc (Toe To Hand – Blink Bonny) was the winner of the Ladbroke Sporting Sprint at Monmore, and Dragon Knight (New Level – Santa Rita) won the Ellen Killen Standard at the same track. There was an All England Cup win at Brough Park for Endon Tiger (Slaneyside Hare – Kevalnig Kwik), who recorded 29.10 for the 480m trip, and King Oscar (Polnoon Chief – Keston Queen) enjoyed a great season, winning the Caffreys New Track Trophy at Monmore, plus the Quicksilver Stakes and the Golden Sprint at Romford.

The year would not be complete without an East Anglian Derby win, and this time it was Terrydrum Kate (Amidus Slippy – Rathbeg Crystal) who took honours at the seaside track. Terrydrum Kate crossed the line in 28.28 for the 462m course.

Charlie said: "She was a lovely bitch with good, early pace. I would say that 460m was as far as she wanted to go, but she excelled over that trip."

CHAPTER THREE

TOP OF THE TREE

Every greyhound trainer wants to win the Derby, and most see it as the culmination of their ambitions if they claim the sport's greatest prize. In only a few years of training full-time, Charlie Lister was already entering the record books. Some Picture had come within a whisker of winning the Scottish, English and Irish Derbies in one year, Spring Rose had achieved the remarkable double of winning the Grand Prix and the St. Leger in the same year, and many of the major competitions had been won by Lister-trained dogs.

FULFILLING POTENTIAL

Far from being content to rest on his laurels, Charlie was only just getting into his stride as a trainer of top-class greyhounds. For him, it is not just the thrill of winning, it is the satisfaction of working with a dog and getting the best out of him.

"I like to see a dog come into my kennel and gradually improve. I see my job as making the most of a dog so that he can run to the best of his potential.

"I try and watch all my dogs run, although sometimes there are conflicts, and I have to decide which dog I should go and see. Sometimes it's a matter of pleasing the owners, sometimes it's a matter of where I'm needed most." But you will never see Charlie in the restaurant, watching the racing at arm's length.

"Often an owner will say: 'I've got a table in the restaurant, why don't you come and join us?' But I'm far happier on the ground, getting the dog ready and watching them race from the trackside."

Charlie gets on well with his owners, and he sees them as being a vital part of his successful set-up. For the most part, the owners leave the decision-making to him.

"They don't want to get involved in the day-to-day running of the kennel, and I live too far away for many of them to come to see their dogs. For example, Mick McCormack, owner of Clear Run, lives in Guernsey, so he doesn't get too involved with what is going on in the kennels.

"Most of the owners like to see their dogs run in a big competition. The goal is to have a dog run in the Derby, and, even if they know their dog has not got a great chance, they still want to enter him. I try to be truthful about a dog's chances. After all, there is no point in wasting £250 on the entry fee if the dog is not good enough. But owners like the big occasion – and some are happy enough just to see their dog run in the Derby heats."

WINNING WAYS

A successful kennel can be built on the reputation of one or two outstanding greyhounds, but a kennel that relies

entirely on open racers must keep moving forwards. As good dogs retire, newcomers must be waiting in the wings. Charlie takes a deep interest in every dog in his kennel, and he is always plotting for the next big race win. As Some Picture was retired to stud, the Mudros kennel was already focused on the racing calendar ahead. In 1998, Dans Sport (New Level – Any Band) proved top class over six bends, winning the Grand Prix at Walthamstow. He followed this up by taking the Racing Post Festival Stayers Stakes at the same track.

"He was a big black dog – a wide runner with lots of early pace. The 640m at Walthamstow was just about as far as he could go, but he certainly ran the track well. He was maybe just short of top class, but he was a good, genuine dog."

Drumsna Power (Ashbury Park – Drumsna Beauty) proved to be a useful bitch for the kennel. Her best win was the Stayers Grand over 647m at Belle Vue. The brindled bitch started at 3-1 and beat Humble Rover by 2¼ lengths, in a time of 40.58.

Farloe Bonus (Alpine Minister – Farloe Post) is an outstanding example of a greyhound that maintained top-class form over an extended period of time. The

FACT FILE

Dans Sport contests the semi-finals of the 1998 Grand Prix.

Dans Sport
- bk dog
- July 1996
- Born: Ireland
- Breeder/owner:
  Jospeh Murphy

New Level

Any Band

Murlens Slippy

Well Plucked

Cooladine Super

Rag Band

Im Slippy

Murlens Chill

One To Note

Soda Pop

Tranquility Sea

Cooladine Ruby

Not Available

Not Available

Dans Sport joined Charlie Lister's kennel at the start of 1998 after winning a confined 29.00 final at Limerick in 29.49. He then contested the Milton Keynes Summer Cup where he finished second to kennelmate Farloe Bonus.

The big challenge was the Laurent Perrier Grand Prix, and Dans Sport won his opening round, and then came second in the next. Drawn in trap 6 for the £7,500 decider, Dans Sport started 6-1, with all the money going on Honest Lord, who was the 5-2 on favourite. But as the boxes went up, Honest Lord missed his break, and it was Farloe Bramble who was first to show. Going into the first bend, Honest Lord picked up pace, but it was Dans Sport who showed the best turn of foot. He steered wide round the first and second bends, but he kept on terms and was ahead at the third.

Showing a tremendous burst of speed, Dans Sport opened up a four-length lead, and, despite game efforts by Honest Lord, the race was over. Dans Sport won in 39.79, with Honest Lord ¾ of a length behind.

1998 ENGLISH GRAND PRIX: FINAL RESULT

Fin.	Name	Sex	Sire	Dam	Time	Dist.	Box	Sp.
1st	Dans Sport	M	New Level	Any Band	39.79		6	6-1
2nd	Honest Lord	M	Coalbrook Tiger	Get Plaid	39.85	¾	1	2-5f
3rd	Scart Eight	M	Connells Cross	Bower Jewel	39.95	1¼	4	25-1
4th	Farloe Bonus	M	Alpine Minister	Farloe Post	40.09	1¾	5	471
5th	Farloe Bramble	M	Michaels Machine	Must Stay	40.49	5	3	16-1
NR	Lydpal Frankie	F	Frightful Flash	Ladys Guest				

white and brindle dog opened his account in 1998 by winning the Summer Cup at Milton Keynes, and went on win the competition in 1999 and 2000. He took honours in the William Hill Stayers Classic at Sheffield in 1999, and finished his career with victory in the MDC Alvin PR Applause Stakes at Hove in 2001. He started at 11-4 and beat Blues Best Tayla by 3¾ lengths in a time of 41.85 for the 695m.

Gaytime Dean (Deenside Joker – Gaytime Steffi) won the Christmas Cracker at Milton Keynes, and Terrydrum Kate recorded her second big competition win when taking the Northern Oaks at Belle Vue. She started as the 11-4 on favourite, and won in 28.53 for the 460m course, beating Impulsive Girl by 1¼ lengths.

The greyhound that proved outstanding in 1999 was Derbay Flyer (Ayr Flyer-Brown Missile) who pulled off a magnificent treble by winning the Birmingham Cup at Perry Barr, the William Hill Laurels at Belle Vue, and the All England Cup at Brough Park – all within a period of four months.

FACT FILE

Derbay Flyer (trap 2) takes the 1999 Laurels on the line.

Derbay Flyer
- f dog
- May 1997
- Born: Ireland
- Breeder: Hugh West
- Owners: George Gibson and Peter Williamson

Ayr Flyer

  Ardfert Sean
- Easy And Slow
- Kielduff Fun

  Slaneyside Glory
- Echo Spark
- Prince Of Rocks

Brown Missile

  Penny Less
- Murlens Slippy
- Penny More

  French Missile
- White Ferrari
- Irish Lace

Derbay Flyer gave a stunning display of speed in the semi-finals of the Group Two Birmingham Cup at Perry Barr when he smashed the track record for the 480m course by 11 spots. He led from the traps, and never looked in any danger as he stormed home in 28.80, beating Knockanoe Rover by almost four lengths.

In the final, the fawn son of Ayr Flyer maintained his unbeaten record in the competition to win the £6,000 prize. He was 6-4 on at the off, and it was Crack Off who led from the traps. Derbay Flyer gave his supporters a fright when he skewed coming out of the boxes, but he was soon back on course, and by the halfway stage he was in front. He still had to hold off a renewed challenge by Crack Off, and was just half a

length in front on the line, recording a time of 29.09.

The next big test came the following month with the William Hill-sponsored Laurels at Belle Vue. In the final, Derbay Flyer was backed from 6-4 into 10-11, but it turned out to be a hard-fought race. Brickfield Bonus, running from trap five, took the lead, and Derbay Flyer just got up on the line to win by a head, clocking 27.80 for the 465m.

In December, Charlie aimed him for his third Group Two competition – the All England Cup at Brough Park. The May 97 whelp continued his tremendous run of form, and was an easy winner of the £5,000 final. Drawn in trap one, he finished 4½ lengths in front of El General, recording 28.79 for the 480m course.

1999 BIRMINGHAM CUP: FINAL RESULT

Fin.	Name	Sex	Sire	Dam	Time	Dist.	Box	Sp.
1st	Derbay Flyer	M	Ayr Flyer	Brown Missile	29.06		1	4-6f
2nd	Crack Off	M	Mountleader Peer	Highsted Rose	29.08	¼	5	5-1
3rd	Kegans Glory	M	Staplers Jo	Miss Kegan	29.16	1	4	7-2
4th	Smoking Bullet	M	Joyful Tidings	Aggies Vixen	29.26	1¼	6	12-1
5th	Knockanroe Rover	M	Mountleader Peer	Seanos Miss	29.40	1¾	2	7-1
6th	Silver Charm	M	Trade Official	Full Of Chat	29.42	SH	3	25-1

1999 WILLIAM HILL LAURELS: FINAL RESULT

Fin.	Name	Sex	Sire	Dam	Time	Dist.	Box	Sp.
1st	Derbay Flyer	M	Ayr Flyer	Brown Missile	27.80		2	10-11f
2nd	Brickfield Bonus	M	Polnoon Chief	Kehers First	27.82	HD	5	3-1
3rd	Terrydrum Flyer	M	Ayr Flyer	Terrydrum Flow	27.90	1	6	1172
4th	Shabbas Mate	M	Slaneyside Hare	Pearls Girl	28.40	6¼	1	12-1
5th	Wath Serenade	M	Justright Melody	Wath Poppy	28.44	½	4	8-1
6th	Water Ranger	M	Come On Ranger	Warren Duchess	28.60	2	3	33-1

1999 ALL ENGLAND CUP: FINAL RESULT

Fin.	Name	Sex	Sire	Dam	Time	Dist.	Box	Sp.
1st	Derbay Flyer	M	Ayr Flyer	Brown Missile	28.79		1	4-6f
2nd	El General	M	Indian Harbour	Minstrel Lady	29.15	4½	6	4-1
3rd	First Opus		Ready About NGA	Rathoona Lass	29.33	2¼	3	16-1
4th	True Reward	M	Dew Reward	Oran Katie	29.34	NS	2	16-1
5th	Laughan Gale	M	Slaneyside Hare	Have A Cigar	29.58	3	5	4-1
NR	Plasterscene Gem	M	Frightful Flash	Fly Smasher				

Charlie said: "I saw him running at Nottingham when he was a puppy, and then the owners brought him to me.

"He looked to be a nice dog, and he showed a lot of improvement. He was a railer. He trapped well, and showed good early pace. He was a lovely dog with a really kind temperament. He was a good kenneller and a good traveller, and that made him easy to train.

"He was a bit like a child – he would give his paw when he was asked, and he always loved being made a fuss of."

In the same year, Foxcover Lizzie (I'm His – Forever Susan) stormed home to a nine-length victory in the Regal Stayers at Shawfield, and Gulleen Slaney (Slaneyside Hare – Gulleen Elsa) won the National Sprint Championship at Nottingham. Gulleen Slaney's victory, which was recorded in 16.07 for the 300m, was even more memorable, as, that Christmas Eve, afternoon Charlie notched up five winners in total, with Sexy Delight, Alannas Spark,

Victory party for Kit Kat Kid, winner of the 1999 Coldseal Puppy Classic at Nottingham. Pictured (left to right): Charlie, and owners Geoff May, Tom Watson, Andy Marsh, Jim Daly (head man), and Steve Spiteri.

Pretty Pleasing and Farloe Bonus winning supporting opens.

Kit Kat Kid, a son of Some Picture, showed something of his sire's magnificent pace in winning the Group One Coldseal Puppy Classic at Nottingham. Starting as the 10-11 favourite, the black dog recorded a time of 30.56 for the £10,000 decider over 500m. He followed this up by winning a Juvenile Invitation at Sheffield.

1999 PUPPY CLASSIC: FINAL RESULT

Fin.	Name	Sex	Sire	Dam	Time	Dist.	Box	Sp.
1st	Kit Kat Kid	M	Some Picture	With A Vengeance	30.56		6	10-11f
2nd	Magna Lane	M	Come On Ranger	Warren Duchess	30.62	¾	3	11-4
3rd	Droopys Sensini	M	Some Picture	Droopys Aine	30.68	¾	2	12-1
4th	Micks Lotto	M	Mountleader Peer	Tracys Lady	30.70	SH	1	9-2
5th	Budd Keizer	M	Shanless Slippy	Minnies Surprise	30.76	¾	5	20-1
6th	Rapid Ranger	M	Come On Ranger	Rapid Vienna	30.77	SH	2	25-1

Lissenair Luke: Bought for a knockdown price, he went on to win the 1999 Scurry Gold Cup.

Hall Green proved to be a profitable venue when Alannas Spark (Summerhill Gift – Persian Spark) won the Midland Oaks in 29.22 for the 480m trip, and, in November, Westmead Striker (Daleys Denis – Westmead Chick) won the Group Three Midland Flat, recording 28.46 for the standard distance.

Colwins Glory (Colwin – Riverstick Maid), a fawn dog whelped in September 1996, started at 5-2 for the Joseph W. Burley Spring Cup at Sheffield, and beat Casseys Shadow by 2¼ lengths, in a time of 29.67 for the 500m.

Lissenair Luke (Ardfert Dan – Suir Dew) proved to be a top-class sprinter, winning a series of open races, including the Group Three William Hill Scurry Gold Cup at Catford. The fawn dog was drawn in trap three for the decider, and justified his 3-1 favouritism, crossing the line in a time of 23.49 for the 385m course.

"He was an early-paced railer who won a total of 32 open races – not bad when you consider he was bought out of Perry Barr sales for 100 guineas! The owners went to the sales and they saw Lissenair Luke being tipped over at the bend. He had no form in Ireland – or what there was, was rubbish – and they got him for 100 guineas.

"He had a few runs at Monmore, and he didn't do anything over four bends. We tried him sprinting, and it was a different story, so we kept him over that distance. In reality, 400 yards was as far as he could get. As you would expect, he was a good trapper with lots of early pace."

1999 SCURRY GOLD CUP: FINAL RESULT

Fin.	Name	Sex	Sire	Dam	Time	Dist.	Box	Sp.
1st	Lissenair Luke	M	Ardfert Dan	Suir Dew	23.49		4	3-1jf
2nd	Union Decree	M	Trade Union	Travelling Light	23.87	4¾	5	9-2
3rd	Kilbarry Boy	M	Mustang Jack	Gold Barbara	23.89	¼	1	8-1
4th	Farncombe Pat	M	Ardfert Dan	Brown Betty	23.91	SH	6	7-1
5th	Lauragh Exile	M	Come On Ranger	Lauragh Enigma	24.29	4¾	3	3-1jf
6th	Bewdley Breeze	M	Cry Dalcash	April Snow	24.31	¼	3	9-2

Rapid Ranger: An exciting prospect for Charlie's kennel.

ENTER RAPID RANGER

When a great greyhound is placed with a great trainer, the result can be remarkable. This proved to be the case when Rapid Ranger (Come On Ranger – Rapid Vienna) joined Charlie Lister's kennel in 1999 – and the rest, as they say, is history.

"Rapid Ranger had been racing in the UK, and I first saw him run at Nottingham. Then I was at Sheffield, and he beat my dog by nine lengths in a good time. I rated my dog – and he wasn't lame – and so I thought, 'This dog's a bit special'.

"He was supposed to be sold that night, but, two days later, I read in the paper that the sale had not gone through. Ray White was keen to buy the dog, so I got hold of the phone number and rang the owner. He said that £15,000 had been offered for the dog, but it hadn't been accepted. I asked what was their rock-bottom price, and I was told £20,000. I rang Ray, and he said: 'Give it to them'. He didn't want any messing around.

"I asked them to bring the dog to Nottingham and I examined him there. I offered £17,000 if we struck the deal straightaway in cash. So I reckon we got a pretty good bargain. At this stage, Rapid Ranger was about 18 months old.

"We gave him a race, and then we took him to Swindon for a competition. He won the first round, but I was not happy with him. I didn't think he ran as well as he should have done. We came to the final, and it was obvious that something was wrong, even though he had no injury. I checked him all over, and, when I looked down his throat, I saw that his tonsils were inflamed. I didn't know whether to chance him in the final. Anyway, we did, and he got beat. Straight after that, he had his tonsils removed and he never looked back."

TOP HONOURS

Rapid Ranger was fit and well, and his campaign was carefully plotted for the 2000 season.

"His first race back was the Scottish Derby. He ran well in the first round and I knew he would only improve. He reached the final and finished in third place. We didn't do much with him until the English Derby, and he was in cracking form. I was always confident that he would win the final. The next stop was the Irish Derby. He got through to the final, but he was unlucky with his trap draw.

"Rapid Ranger was the perfect dog to train. He always looked well – his coat gleamed. The best thing about him was that he was so laid back. He slept in his kennel before racing as if he didn't have a care in the world. You would often see him lying on his back with all four legs in the air. Then, when you brought him out of the kennel, he was calm but alert. I remember, when it was his turn to parade in front of the TV cameras on Derby final night, he took his place, and then gave himself a good shake, and then moved on!

"He was an early-paced railer, but he could run out of traps two and three. In fact, in trap one, I always thought he moved out a stride. He didn't trap as well out of one, whereas he flew out of traps two and three. He didn't trap to the sound of the hare, he trapped to the lids, and that was why he was not affected by the Derby roar. He still got his break because he didn't need to listen to the hare. He flew out as soon as the lids went up."

OTHER SUCCESSES

Rapid Ranger grabbed the media's attention, but there were other outstanding performances from Lister-trained runners. Parliament Act (Trade Official – Lemon Ashling) showed tremendous pace, winning the Northern Sprint at Sheffield. The brindled dog, starting at a generous 6-1, crossed the line 2½ lengths in front, clocking 16.38 for the 280m.

"Parliament Act had been running four bends, but he didn't really get the distance. In his first few races with me, he was a bit unlucky, but there were certainly no flashy runs. However, I believed in him; I just thought he needed a few more runs to come right. At the start of the competition at Sheffield, I thought he would win, even though no one else did. He started at 8-1 and was an easy winner. People must have thought that was a bit of a fluke because he was 6-1 for the final. But he went on to win, and broke the track record."

Toblermorey Boy: An easy winner of the 2000 All England Cup.

Toblermorey Boy (Spiral Nikita – Lemon Polly) won a Juvenile Stakes at Sheffield over 500m, and followed up by winning the Group Two All England Cup at Brough Park. Drawn in trap six, he gave his backers little cause for concern, leading from the half-way stage and crossing the line 6¼ lengths ahead of Calypso Cole in a time of 30.34

There was a Group Three win at Hall Green when Wise Emerald (Trade Official – Try A Minnie) collected the Midland Flat.

The brindle and white dog started at 4-1, and won in a fast 28.31 for the 480m course, beating Derbay Pride by 3 lengths.

2000 ALL ENGLAND CUP: FINAL RESULT

Fin.	Name	Sex	Sire	Dam	Time	Dist.	Box	Sp.	Comment
1st	Toblermorey Boy	M	Spiral Nikita	Lemon Polly	28.68		6	1-2f	ep, led ½
2nd	Calypso Cole	M	Thorgil Tex	Wath Poppy	29.18	6¼	1	3-1	crd2
3rd	Winter Ray	M	Longvalley Manor	Barefoot Music	29.30	1½	3	20-1	crd2
4th	Haywire Spark	M	Ratify	Crossleigh Spark	29.64	4¼	2	33-1	fcd ck2
5th	El Joker	M	Deenside Joker	Code Dancer	29.78	1¾	5	5-1	q aw, b blk3
6th	Allhandsondeck	M	Staplers Jo	Lisas Cool		DIST	4	10-1	crd2, blk& fell3

2000 MIDLAND FLAT CHAMPIONSHIP: FINAL RESULT

Fin.	Name	Sex	Sire	Dam	Time	Dist.	Box	Sp.	Comment
1st	Wise Emerald	M	Trade Official	Try A Minnie	28.31		6	4-1	mid w, ld ¼
2nd	Derbay Pride	M	Westmead Merlin	Woodford Special	28.55	3	2	11-2	rls, crd1
3rd	Blue Tex	M	Thorgil Tex	Dons Pride	28.59	½	1	ev. f	s aw, ep, mid, crd1
4th	Broadacres Butch	M	Top Honcho	Broadacres Star	28.71	1½	3	7-1	s aw, mid, bmp2
5th	Kincraig Billy	F	Spiral Nikita	Dazzlem Danoi	28.79	1	5	12-1	wide, crd1
6th	Toms The One	M	Toms The Best	Celtic Lady	28.89	1¼	4	6-1	rls, bmp1, crd ¾

Sexy Delight: A home-bred star.

But the greyhound that Charlie was most interested in was Sexy Delight, the product of the home-bred litter of Charlie's two great stars, Some Picture and Spring Rose. He said: "She proved to be an outstanding stayer. Although she was a marathon bitch, she had good pace. She could come from behind, or win from in front. She was also a brainy bitch, always looking around to see what was going on. If she was in the kennel, and you came in to talk to her, she would tip her head to one side, as if she was listening to you."

The black bitch was a prolific open race winner. Her most notable victory was the £6,000 TV Trophy at Wimbledon, which she won in 54.51, beating Spenwood Wizard by a head. The following year she recorded wins in the Teamtal.com Trophy at Hove, and the Stow Marathon at Walthamstow. Sadly, she was diagnosed with cancer.

2000 EVENING STANDARD TV TROPHY: FINAL RESULT

Fin.	Name	Sex	Sire	Dam	Time	Dist.	Box	Sp.
1st	Sexy Delight	F	Some Picture	Spring Rose	54.51		1	9-4f
2nd	Spenwood Wizard	F	Larryandy	Spenwood Magic	54.53	sh. hd	6	3-1
3rd	Hollinwood Poppy	F	Dempsey Duke	Hollinwood Major	54.81	3½	5	3-1
4th	Drumsna Cross	F	Asbury Park	Drumsna Beauty	54.91	1¼	2	33-1
5th	El Poker	M	Come On Ranger	Good Customer	55.01	1¼	3	8-1
6th	Spenwood Gem	F	Larryandy	Spenwood Magic	55.03	¼	4	4-1

TRAGIC BLOW

In a year of triumphs, there was another tragedy for the kennel when Kit Kat Kid suffered an horrific fall while competing in a 500m open at Sheffield. There was trouble early on in the race when Kit Kat Kid and Farloe Careless were in a barging match, and then Kit Kat Kid fell on the crown of the two bends.

The race was stopped, and the greyhound was carried from the track. After the dog had been sedated, Dave Baldwin (Sheffield's Director of Racing) drove him home, accompanied by one of Charlie's lads, so that the dog would be as comfortable as possible. The next morning, it was found that the shoulder injuries he sustained were inoperable, and Kit Kat Kid had to be put down. Charlie was in Ireland at the time, and he was shattered when he heard the news.

"It was devastating because I really don't think we got to see the best of him. He had had a lot of problems with injuries, and he was only going to improve with more races."

Accidents are an inevitable part of the sport, but that doesn't mean that Charlie finds this aspect of his job easy to cope with.

"The worst is having to ring up an owner and tell them that their dog is injured. Many of my owners are not present at the track, so it's up to me to break the news. I hate doing it – it really gets me down."

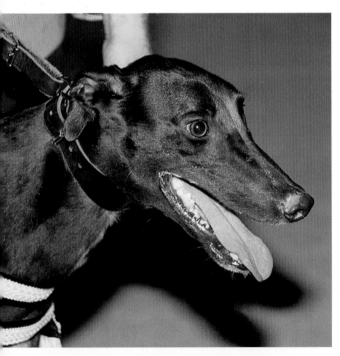

Kit Kat Kid: Victim of a tragic accident.

MAKING HISTORY

At the start of the 2001 season, the big question on everyone's lips was: would Rapid Ranger be brought back for a second tilt at the Greyhound Derby?

"We were making our Derby plans, and Ray asked how Rapid Ranger was. I said, 'He's bouncing – he's knocking down the door.' Ray asked what I thought about attempting a second Derby, and I said I would try him out. He had to be running as well as the previous year for it to make any sense.

"I gave him a gallop at home, and he came storming up. I then gave him a couple of sprint trials, and he was flying. He had always been lightly raced, and I think that was significant. I believe there are only so many races in a dog. It's like the motor in a car – it will only keep running for so long. To my mind, Rapid Ranger was as good as ever, and we decided to have a go.

"He was drawn in trap four for the final, and he did exactly the same time as he recorded in the Derby final the year before. That shows remarkable consistency."

Rapid Ranger became only the third greyhound to win back-to-back Derbies when he pulled off the double in 2001. The other dual winners were Mick The Miller in 1929 and 1930, and Patricias Hope in 1972 and 1973. But Rapid Ranger was the only dog to have the same owner/trainer combination for both events. What do such records mean to Charlie?

Making history: Owner Ray White holds the trophy aloft, celebrating Rapid Ranger's second Derby win.

**Parliament Act:
A top-class
sprinter.**

"I think the media are more interested in records than I am. I want to see my greyhounds perform at their very best, and I love to win – but there's always another day, and another competition, to prepare for."

TOP PERFORMANCES

If you read the sporting newspapers in 2001, you would have been forgiven for thinking Rapid Ranger was the only greyhound in Charlie Lister's kennel. But that was not the way Charlie saw it. He has always taken a keen interest in every single dog in his care, and he gives them all the best of his attention.

"If you are going to be successful, you have to be interested in every dog you handle, and I always want to be there to see them race."

In 2001, open race winners came thick and fast, and there was scarcely a major competition without a Lister-trained greyhound in contention. The year got off to a flying start when Charlie took a strong team of greyhounds to Hove at the end of March to take part in the Trainers Championship. With dogs of the calibre of Rapid Ranger, Parliament Act and True Honcho, Charlie took the Championship in style.

In May, Call Me Baby (Popov – Masonbrook Annie), owned by Ray White, won the Midland Oaks at Hall Green in

2001 GOLD CUP: FINAL RESULT

Fin.	Name	Sex	Sire	Dam	Time	Dist.	Box	Sp.	Comment
1st	El Ronan	M	Staplers Jo	Freds Flame	27.10		1	4-6f	led 1st
2nd	Kingsbrook Lea	M	Come On Ranger	Courage Queen	27.14	½	4	4-1	q aw, led to 1st
3rd	El Zita	F	Lassa Java	Bellingham Rosi	27.20	¾	6	7-1	fin wll
4th	Kiln Wood	M	Lassa Java	Carriglea Judy	27.62	5¼	5	14-1	s aw, wide
5th	Calypso Cole	M	Thorgil Tex	Wath Poppy	27.64	hd	2	8-1	svd to run up
6th	Droopys Clay	M	Some Picture	Rebeccas Charm	27.66	sh hd	3	16-1	clr run

traps-to-line style, hanging on by a head to beat Kinda Swell. Parliament Act continued his winning ways, taking the Pepsi Cola Sprint at Yarmouth, clocking 16.71 for the 277m trip.

"Parliament Act broke five track records in his career (Sheffield 280m, Belle Vue 237m, Nottingham 300m, Hove 285m and Monmore 264m), and he was Best Sprinter in the annual awards. He was a good starter, and he had fantastic early pace. He could leave other dogs for dead going to the corner."

There were also some promising performances from youngsters, with Droopys Prowler (Droopys Merson – Lisnakill Vicki) winning the £3,000 Racing Post Puppy Stakes at Walthamstow and the Christmas Puppy Cracker at Monmore, and Farloe Totty (Plasterscene Gem – Listen To Reason) winning the Puppy Cesarewitch at Peterborough. El Ronan (Staplers Jo – Freds Flame) proved to be an admirably consistent greyhound

for the kennel and enjoyed a great season. He took the honours in the East Anglian Challenge at Yarmouth, and, within a few weeks, he was contesting the Group One Gold Cup at Oxford. Starting as 6-4 on favourite, he led from the first bend and crossed the line in 27.10 for the 450m course.

ILLNESS STRIKES

It was January 2002, and Charlie had been to Walthamstow to see Sexy Delight win her semi-final of the Pepsi Cola Marathon. After the long drive back to South Clifton, Charlie was understandably tired, but there was no other cause for concern. He had a cup of coffee and went to bed.

At 2.30 in the morning, he awoke, but when he tried to get out of bed, he couldn't move his left leg.

"At first I thought it was cramp, and I tried rubbing my leg, but I quickly realised it was something more serious. I woke Pat and got her to call an ambulance. It was on the way to the hospital that I started to feel really frightened – I just didn't know what was happening."

A stroke was diagnosed, and Charlie was kept in hospital for a fortnight. Unsurprisingly, he was not the easiest of patients.

"To begin with, I couldn't move and I didn't want to do anything. I could only walk if I was supported by the physio. But after a week I started to get fed up. I saw a zimmer frame at the end of my bed, and decided I would have a try on that. That didn't go down very well – they said I had to have a nurse to help me. I started practising on the zimmer, and I just kept walking up and down the ward. I was determined to get going."

The staff at the hospital were equally keen to have him back on his feet as he grew increasingly impatient to return to Mudros. When one of his dogs was running, Charlie took up a position at the entrance of the hospital so that he could use his mobile and receive an on-the-spot commentary from one of the kennel lads.

"We had quite a few winners, and the lads coped really well – but I couldn't wait to get back. I got so that I could walk with a stick, and, when I proved I could walk up stairs, I was allowed home. The first time I went racing, I walked with a stick, but I felt that everyone was looking at me. I came home and I said to Pat: 'You'd better chuck that stick out – I'm not using it again.'

"The doctor said I should take some time off after I had got over the stroke. I have never been much of one for holidays, and I had never been abroad before, but Pat and I decided to go to Portugal for 12 days. That was too long, and I started to get bored. It was alright for five or six days, but then I wanted to get back."

Back at home, Charlie has tried to take things a bit easier. "The lads let the dogs out first thing in the morning, but I still like to be there to prepare the breakfasts. Apart from that, I carry on as I always did. The only difference is that Pat and I take a holiday once a year. Last time, we went to Cyprus for a week, and that wasn't too bad – actually I quite enjoyed it."

ONE MORE TIME?

Charlie was very much back in charge by the spring of 2002, and his top priority was assessing likely candidates for the derby.

"When Rapid Ranger won his second Greyhound Derby, he was retired to stud, and there was no thought of him making a comeback.

In flying form, Rapid Ranger contesting the second round of the 2001 Greyhound Derby.

Rapid Ranger
- brindle dog
- January 1998
- Born: Ireland
- Breeder: Martin Broughan
- Owner: Raymond White

Come On Ranger

Greenpark Fox
- Citizen Supreme
- Stern Satoo

Mandies Handbag
- Im Slippy
- Lindas Dance

Rapid Vienna

Lodge Prince
- Sand Man
- Cooga Customer

Vienna Girl
- Yellow Band
- Springfield Lady

Rapid Ranger's career did not have the most promising of starts, with a graded B6 defeat at Stainforth under his then owner-trainer Mike Pomfrett. But he started to show what he was made of when he reached the finals of the Manchester Puppy Cup at Belle Vue and the Coldseal Puppy Classic at Nottingham. He finished in sixth place in the Nottingham Group One final, which was won by the Lister-trained Kit Kat Kid. But the brindled son of Come On Ranger had done enough to attract serious interest, and, after winning the Dransfield Lotteries Puppy Cup at Sheffield, he changed hands. He became the property of Ray White, and was sent straight to Charlie Lister's kennel.

Charlie was ready to be patient with his new recruit, and was unperturbed by early defeats at Walthamstow and Swindon. He waited until the Scottish Derby to give the greyhound his first major test. Rapid Ranger looked to be improving as the competition progressed, and, drawn in trap three in the final, he finished in third place with Knockeevan Star the 29.19 winner.

The next stop was Plough Lane, and a tilt at the 2000 Greyhound Derby. Rapid Ranger moved through the rounds of the premier event. He was defeated in the second round, and in the semi-finals, but he was still made favourite for the decider. He was drawn in trap two, and recording a 5.11 sectional, he was never in any danger. He coasted home with 3½ lengths to spare from runner-up Rackethall Jet. His winning time was 28.71.

It was on to the Select Stakes at Nottingham, and this time Rackethall Jet got his revenge and beat the Derby winner by a neck. The Irish Derby was the next goal. Rapid Ranger acquitted himself well,

finishing runner-up to Judicial Pride, despite the disadvantage of a trap five draw in the final. Charlie has always believed in confining top-class dogs to the major competitions, and Rapid Ranger had a seven-month break before preparing for a second tilt at the Derby. His comeback race was at Hove where he finished second behind Droopys Vieri. Then it was a second attempt at the Scottish Derby, but in the second round he made his exit when Droopys Vieri again got the better of him. At this stage, there were some doubters, but Charlie was confident that he had Rapid Ranger ready for a second tilt at the Greyhound Derby. There were defeats in the first round and the quarter-finals, but Rapid Ranger was clearly saving his best until last. Despite his trap four draw, Charlie was optimistic in the run-up to the final.

"We go into the race with no pressure whatsoever. He's proven he is a champion by reaching four derby finals, and whether he wins this one or not, he will still be a truly great dog. He is as fit and well as ever, and although he has a tough draw to overcome, if he hits the boxes the way he can, I think he could lead at the first corner."

Sonic Flight was the red-hot favourite for the decider, but the much-talked-about contest between him and Rapid Ranger failed to materialise. Rapid Ranger, starting at 7-4, flew out of the traps, leaving Sonic Flight to negotiate crowding at the start and at the first bend. He crossed the winning line in 28.71 – exactly the same time as he had recorded in the Derby final the previous year. Sonic Flight finished in second place, 3¼ lengths adrift. Now a double derby winner, Rapid Ranger was elected to the Greyhound Hall of Fame – the third Lister-trained greyhound to achieve this honour.

2000 SCOTTISH DERBY: FINAL RESULT

Fin.	Name	Sex	Sire	Dam	Time	Dist.	Box	Sp.
1st	Knockeevan Star	M	Slaneyside Hare	Rubys Bridge	29.19		1	3-1
2nd	Ryefield Snowy	F	Some Picture	Faultless Lady	29.35	2	4	20-1
3rd	Rapid Ranger	M	Come On Ranger	Rapid Vienna	29.37	¼	3	3-1
4th	Knockanroe Rover	M	Mountleader Peer	Seanos Miss	29.39	sh hd	2	2-1f
5th	Fat Boy Slim	M	Some Picture	Elbony Violet	29.55	2	5	7-2
6th	Springtime	F	Vintage Prince	Meantime	29.91	4½	6	4-1

2000 ENGLISH DERBY: FINAL RESULT

Fin.	Name	Sex	Sire	Dam	Time	Dist.	Box	Sp.
1st	Rapid Ranger	M	Come On Ranger	Rapid Vienna	28.71		2	7-4f
2nd	Rackethall Jet	M	Mountleader Peer	Tracys Lady	28.97	3¼	3	7-1
3rd	Greenfield Deal	M	Spiral Nikita	Dainty Model	29.11	1¾	4	14-1
4th	Deerfield Sunset	M	Vintage Prince	Sunset Blonde	29.13	hd	1	2-1
5th	Smoking Bullet	M	Joyful Tidings	Aggies Vixen	29.65	6½	5	8-1
6th	Farloe Club	M	April Trio	Farloe Dancer	29.81	2	6	3-1

2000 IRISH DERBY: FINAL RESULT

Fin.	Name	Sex	Sire	Dam	Time	Dist.	Box	Sp.
1st	Judicial Pride	M	Thorgil Tex	Dons Pride	29.68		2	6-4f
2nd	Rapid Ranger	M	Come On Ranger	Rapid Vienna	29.89	3	5	7-4
3rd	Miss Tetley	F	Staplers Jo	Much Better	29.94	¾	6	12-1
4th	Ballyhoe Cyclone	M	Lassa Java	Picture Palace	30.22	4	3	33-1
5th	Golfing Lad	M	Polnoon Chief	Roses Jewel	30.36	2	4	33-1
6th	Currie Kid	M	Spiral Nikita	Westmead Spirit	30.54	2½	1	6-1

2001 ENGLISH DERBY: FINAL RESULT

Fin.	Name	Sex	Sire	Dam	Time	Dist.	Box	Sp.	Comment
1st	Rapid Ranger	M	Come On Ranger	Rapid Vienna	28.71		4	7-4	soon ld
2nd	Sonic Flight	M	Frightful Flash	Westmead Flight	28.97	3½	3	10-11f	crd st, bmp1
3rd	Castlelyons Dani	M	Spiral Nikita	Foxclose Daisy	29.09	1½	2	14-1	crd2&3
4th	Countrywide Tams	F	Lassa Java	Persian Spark	29.11	hd	1	14-1	ep , rls
5th	Smoking Bullet	M	Joyful Tidings	Aggies Vixen	29.39	3½	5	10-1	crd1
6th	Droopys Honcho	M	Top Honcho	Droopys Fergie	29.41	hd	6	7-1	bmp1

"Ray is not in it for the money. He leaves the decisions about racing up to me. We both had it in our minds that Rapid Ranger's racing career was at an end.

"We were at the Greyhound Awards dinner, and we were having a drink at the bar. There were television people around, recording interviews. For a joke, Ray said we were thinking about having third tilt at the Derby in 2003. It was all in fun, but the next day he phoned me and asked me what I really thought about the dog's chances.

"I gave him a few trials, and I was confident that he could perform at his best. It was 11 months since he had last raced, but he looked as keen as ever. In fact, he got as far as the third round. There was a lot of trouble in the race, and Rapid Ranger just missed qualifying.

"That year it was a poor final. If Rapid Ranger had got through to the final with that quality of dogs, he would have stood a very good chance. I don't think it tarnished his reputation. He ran well, even though he got beat.

"Rapid Ranger went to stand at stud in Ireland. Ray was so fond of him that he thought about keeping him as a pet. Anyway, it was decided that he would go and stand alongside his father, Come On Ranger.

"When they came to get him, I couldn't take it. I had to go to bed for the rest of the day. I was that broken up."

SUPPORTING CAST

Rapid Ranger's bid for glory in his third Derby ended in the third round, but 2002 proved to be an outstanding year for the kennel, with top-class performances from a number of rising stars. Charlie has formed a fruitful association with Des Loughrey in Ireland, and following Farloe Bonus and Farloe Totty, Farloe Forty joined the kennel strength. A son of Top Honcho, Farloe Forty showed excellent form in winning the Regal Puppy Trophy at Sunderland in February. Drawn in trap one, the black dog led from the second and was a decisive winner, beating Scripino by 6¼ lengths in a time of 27.74 for the 450m. It was a great night for Charlie, who had a total of four winners, including El Ronan, which won the Feature race – the Regal Gold Cup – worth £5,000. Starting as the 9-4 favourite, he led from the start, and was a four-length winner, in a time of 27.47. It was a particularly sweet victory for Charlie, as El Ronan had been badly injured the previous year when contesting the East Anglian Derby, and had been given a long lay-off before returning to the track. El

El Ronan: Winner of the 2002 Regal Gold Cup, and the 2002 Milton Keynes Derby.

Ronan stayed in sparkling form throughout the year, and in November he was back in the money, winning the £6,000 Milton Keynes Derby. Inevitably, the brindled dog started as favourite, and, in a hard-fought race, he overcame crowding at the third turn to win in 26.68 for the 440m.

"He was a lovely, generous dog, and he won a lot of good races. He had early pace but he also had good back pace. His limit was 460-480m, but he was a determined runner. He was contesting a veterans race at Walthamstow when he injured a gracilis muscle. It wasn't that bad, but at his age I thought it was time to retire him. I didn't want to see him being beaten by lesser dogs."

2002 REGAL GOLD CUP: FINAL RESULT

Fin.	Name	Sex	Sire	Dam	Time	Dist.	Box	Sp.	Comment
1st	El Ronan	M	Staplers Jo	Freds Flame	27.47		4	9-4f	led rn up
2nd	Honchos First	M	Top Honcho	Ardera Melody	27.79	4	5	6-1	crd stt&2
3rd	Harsu Super	M	Ratify	Yes Super	27.81	hd	6	6-1	crd stt
4th	Occhi Gialli	M	Roanokee	Lydpal Cassie	27.99	2¼	3	9-2	b crd1
5th	Farball	M	Macsea Royal	Kokkini Hani	28.05	¾	1	5-2	s aw, b crd2, crd3
6th	Coolagorna Glory	M	Top Honcho	Rathmoy Raver	28.43	4¾	2	6-1	b crd1&3

2002 MILTON KEYNES DERBY: FINAL RESULT

Fin.	Name	Sex	Sire	Dam	Time	Dist.	Box	Sp.	Comment
1st	El Ronan	M	Staplers Jo	Freds Flame	26.68		5	5-2f	ep, rls-mid, crd3
2nd	Tippums Spot	M	Spoonbill Snowey	Bazile Slippy	26.76	1	4	8-1	q aw, rls, ld to run in
3rd	Dubh Soldier	M	Top Honcho	Pollerton Lass	26.98	2¾	3	10-1	rls, blk2
4th	Farloe Forty	M	Top Honcho	Fees Chance	27.04	¾	1	4-1	rls, blk2
5th	Larkhill Lo	M	Larkhill Jo	Merry Bluebell	27.04	d. heat	6	3-1	v s aw, wide
6th	Blue Gooner	M	Staplers Jo	Code Dancer	27.34	3¾	2	3-1	rls, clr run

Seskin Robert, a black dog by Spiral Nikita, notched up a series of open race wins over six bends, and Charlie decided he had the pace to run over four. He proved his trainer right, reaching the finals of the Pall Mall and the Scottish Derby, but in terms of four bend wins, he had to be content with the Ladbrokes Festival 480 at Monmore, which he won by half a length in 28.79.

Toms Autumn (Toms The Best – Autumn Rain) made a promising start to his career when taking the Ladbrokes Dotcom Puppy Trophy at Nottingham. He was an easy winner, beating Royston King by 4¼ lengths in a time of 30.34 for the 500m.

Soviet King, a son of Come On Ranger, took on the best of the sprinters to win the Ladbrokes Freephone Sprint Trophy at Nottingham, and for the stayers it was True Honcho (Top Honcho – Security Special) who scored in the Tomsthebest.com at Hove.

Knockaun Joker (Deenside Joker – Gaytime Steffi) enjoyed a long and illustrious career, and was rarely out of contention over six and eight bends. The fawn dog's best wins were the Dransfield Stayers at Belle Vue over 647m, which he won in 39.87, and the Derby Purse over 659m at Yarmouth, which he won in 41.05.

Charlie had high hopes of Larkhill Bullet (Staplers Jo – Annie Bullet) which were soon justified when the dog won the Northern Sprint at Sheffield. Drawn in trap six, he started at 11-8 on for the

Larkhill Bullet records a stylish victory in the 2002 East Anglian Derby.

Fin.	Name	Sex	Sire	Dam	Time	Dist.	Box	Sp.	Comment
1st	Larkhill Bullet	M	Staplers Jo	Annies Bullet	28.22		6	6-4f	ep, w, fin wll
2nd	Blue Gooner	M	Staplers Jo	Code Dancer	28.49	3½	1	11-4	rls, fin wll
3rd	Paris Wood	M	He Knows	Ballinabola Mar	28.53	½	3	14-1	rls, fin wll
4th	Lincs Lad	M	Thorgil Tex	Slippy Ginger	28.67	1¾	2	14-1	s aw, m
5th	El Ronan	M	Staplers Jo	Freds Flame	28.78	1½	4	10-3	ep, blk2
6th	Droopys Corleone	M	Top Honcho	Droopys Kylie	28.81	nk	5	5-1	blk rls

56th EAST ANGLIAN GREYHOUND DERBY 2002: FINAL RESULT

decider over 280m. There was trouble at the first bend, but Larkhill Bullet showed good finishing pace to win by two lengths in 16.51.

Charlie decided that Larkhill Bullet was ready to step up to four bends, and the brindled dog justified this decision in style, winning the East Anglian Derby – making it six wins in the competition for Lister-trained greyhounds. Larkhill Bullet was the 6-4 favourite, and, despite steering a wide course, he finished 3½ lengths in front, recording 28.22 for the 462m.

DERBY HOPEFULS

As always, Charlie started 2003 with the Derby in mind – and he had never had a stronger team of hopefuls. Burberry Boy (Top Honcho – Faultess Quest) Larkhill Bullet, Micks Mystic (Come On Ranger – Tracys Lady), Farloe Verdict, and the much-vaunted Top Savings (Top Honcho – Too Breezy) were all likely contenders. He looked at each of his dogs, and decided what preparation would be most suitable.

"Micks Mystic had been injured and was off the track for six months. He had been

Burberry Boy (3): One of Charlie's strong hopefuls for the 2003 Derby.

FACT FILE

Micks Mystic: Brought back into racing after a spell at stud.

Micks Mystic
- bk dog
- November 1999
- Born: Ireland
- Breeder: Tracy O'Connor
- Owner: Marie O'Neill

Come On Ranger

Greenpark Fox

Citizen Supreme

Stern Satoo

Mandies Handbag

Im Slippy

Lindas Dance

Tracys Lady

Joyful Tidings

Whisper Wishes

Newmans Mall

Patterdale Toni

Yes Speedy

Ballybrack Charm

icks Mystic, a son of Come On Ranger (sire of Rapid Ranger) came to Charlie Lister's kennel with an outstanding record. In Ireland he was the winner of Cork's Bank Of Ireland Stakes in 28.29, and finished second to Sonic Flight in the Irish Laurels. The black dog had a spell at stud, and, at three and a half years of age, he was brought over to England to resume his racing career.

The big goal was the Greyhound Derby, but Charlie was quick to see that Micks Mystic was raring to go, so he was entered in the Regal Scottish Derby. In the first round, the black dog was caught in the final few strides by Farloe Verdict, but then he reeled off straight wins in 29.28 and 29.24 for the 480m course. Despite a tricky trap five draw, Micks Mystic was made the 6-4 on favourite for the £25,000 decider. Backers hoped that his tremendous early pace would be significant, and this proved to be the case. By the second bend he was in front, and he coasted home five lengths clear of Bomber Graham. His winning time was 29.07 for the 480m course.

2003 REGAL SCOTTISH DERBY: FINAL RESULT

Fin.	Name	Sex	Sire	Dam	Time	Box	Sp.	Comment
1st	Micks Mystic	M	Come On Ranger	Tracys Lady	29.07	5	4-6f	ep, clr2
2nd	Bomber Graham	M	Top Honcho	Faultless Quest	29.47	3	12-1	mid, ev ch
3rd	Unassailable	M	Spiral Nikita	Grayslands Zoom	29.53	1	10-1	mid, blk1
4th	Swift Star	M	Knockeevan Star	Spice Beauty	29.83	6	8-1	b blk1
5th	Sportsman	M	Staplers Jo	Slaneyside Robin	29.97	4	5-1	b blk1
6th	Stay Please	M	Thorgil Tex	Pinetree Betty	30.31	2	10-1	crd rn up, b blk1

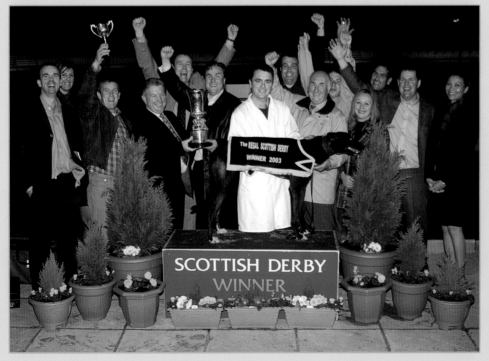

Celebrations as Micks Mystic wins the 2003 Scottish Derby.

Top Savings: He clocked the fastest time in the 2003 English Derby.

retired and mated a few bitches. He seemed well and, after giving him a couple of gallops, his owners decided they wanted to have a go at the English Derby.

"That was a big thing to ask after he had been off for so long, and he was already three and a half. We gave him a couple of trials, and he was absolutely flying round. I said: 'I think this dog is going so well we should try him in the Scottish Derby.' He had very good early pace, and he could run from any box. He was a really good dog.

"He won the Scottish Derby, but then he got injured. The English Derby came too soon for him and he missed qualifying, but he came back on final night and won one of the supporting opens."

The Scottish Derby was planned as the first big test for Farloe Verdict, a black bitch sired by Droopys Vieri out of She Knew.

She came to Charlie with a fast time at Lifford on her card, and soon proved her value when winning the Blue Riband at Hall Green. Charlie rated her chances strongly in the Derby.

"She's a strong running bitch, and she stays on. She always gives 100 per cent – in fact, she's never run a bad race. She's got as good a chance as any."

Top Savings must certainly go down as one of the most talented – and one of the most frustrating – dogs Charlie has ever trained. He came to Mudros with a string of spectacular puppy wins, but he was beset by injury.

"He was brilliant as a puppy, and then he came to me after he was injured. He took a long time to get right. He had a deep muscle injury in his back, and it was hard to treat. He didn't appear to be lame when he

Burberry Boy: Charlie's seventh winner of the East Anglian Derby.

walked, but it showed up at speed.

"We had him for six months before we attempted to race him. He had every sort of treatment, and he came back well, but to my mind, we didn't ever see the best of him again.

"The trouble was that he kept picking up injuries, which made him a very frustrating dog to train. There was one time when I really felt I'd had enough, and I was ready to give up on the dog. It's one thing when a dog is injured when he is in your kennel, but when he comes to you injured, it can be very hard. But I stuck at it, and I did get

him right."

Top Savings started his pre-Derby preparation in fine style, running unbeaten to win the Bookmakers Guineas at Nottingham in April. Despite crashing out of the Scottish Derby in the first round, he opened his Wimbledon account in stunning style, winning by ten lengths in a time of 28.40, which proved to be the fastest time clocked in the competition. Burberry Boy looked in great form until he sustained an injury in the quarter-finals, which meant he could take no further part in the classic. However, he more than made up for this

57th EAST ANGLIAN DERBY 2003: FINAL RESULT

Fin.	Name	Sex	Sire	Dam	Time	Dist.	Box	Sp.	Comment
1st	Burberry Boy	M	Top Honcho	Faultless Quest	28.01		4	ev. f	w, blk stt, ep, fin wll
2nd	Lockup Firedice	M	Cushie Draco	Cushie Flair	28.27	3¼	3	10-1	ep, rls, blk1, fin wll
3rd	Farloe Hack	M	Staplers Jo	Farloe Dingle	28.54	3½	1	2-1	blk1, rls, fin wll
4th	Droopys Corleone	M	Top Honcho	Droopys Kylie	28.81	3½	5	5-1	blk stt, rls
5th	Ard Thunder	M	TomsThe Best	Ard Lightning	28.90	1¼	6	16-1	blk1, mid
6th	Cash The Deal	M	Joannestown Cash	Droopys Andrea	29.05	1¾	2	6-1	blk1 & ½, rls

disappointment later in the year when he made it win number seven for Charlie in the East Anglian Derby at Yarmouth. He started as favourite for the Group One event, and showed his strong finishing pace to win in 28.01 for the 462m – 3¼ lengths in front of Lockup Firedice.

Charlie said: "Burberry Boy was an oldish dog when he came to me. I didn't have him right for the Derby, but after running in some one-off races, he was in cracking form for the East Anglian Derby. He's got lots of early pace and stays the full 480m."

RECORD FINAL

In the third round, Charlie's three Derby prospects – Farloe Verdict, Top Savings and Larkhill Bullet – were drawn in the same heat, but they all got through, and he ended up with three dogs in the final. The kennel had never received so much media attention, and the phone was red-hot for days leading up to the big event. Charlie does not relish the publicity, but he is always ready to co-operate with the press and with Sky TV.

"Sky, in particular, has done so much for greyhound racing, so I think it is important to be as helpful as possible – although there are times when you might prefer some privacy. They are very clever at coming to find you!"

But even when they find Charlie, he is not always as talkative as the interviewer may wish. Sky TV was after a last-minute preview of the Derby final and asked Charlie where he would like to see ante-post favourite Top Savings as they entered the back straight for the 2003 premier event. "Ahead," was Charlie's brief but apposite reply!

There was much speculation as to which of the three dogs Charlie favoured, but typically he gave very little away. "May the best dog win – let's just hope it's one of mine!"

This was not to be Charlie's night. Trouble early on made nonsense of the formbook, and it was Droopys Hewitt, a 16-1 shot, who missed the pile up, and

2003 ENGLISH DERBY: FINAL RESULT

Fin.	Name	Sex	Sire	Dam	Time	Dist.	Box	Sp.	Comment
1st	Droopys Hewitt	M	Top Honcho	Droopys Cheryl	28.82		3	16-1	msd tbl, led1
2nd	Farloe Verdict	F	Droopys Vieri	She Knew	29.12	3¾	2	12-1	badly crd1
3rd	Top Savings	M	Top Honcho	Too Breezy	29.18	¾	6	4-7f	crd run up, b crd1
4th	Farloe Pocket	M	Larkhill Jo	Tornaroy Tumble	29.21	nk	4	33-1	crd stt&1
5th	Man Of Cash	M	Cool Performance	Travelling Light	29.47	3¾	1	3-1	crd1&3
6th	Larkhill Bullet	M	Staplers Jo	Annies Bullet	29.49	sh hd	5	6-1	crd stt& rn up &1

was first past the post. Trained by Andy Ioannou, he recorded a time of 28.82, with Farloe Verdict the runner-up, 3¾ lengths adrift. Top Savings, the 7-4 on favourite, came third, and Larkhill Bullet finished in sixth place.

"I really thought I had chances with all of them – and with three in the final, I thought I had a very good chance of winning.

"If Top Savings had led to the bend, it would have been all over – he had that much pace, nothing could pick him up. There is no doubt that he was the fastest dog in the Derby. But he found a load of trouble, and there was nothing he could do.

"Of course I was disappointed with the result. When you have three dogs in the final, you know you have every chance. But when you get beaten fair and square, you have to accept it – and you must be the first to congratulate the winner."

POST DERBY

Charlie is not the type to waste his time with regrets, and he was soon plotting the next races for his top-class team. He entered Top Savings in the Ladbroke Gold Cup at Monmore, but again, he proved unlucky. In the semi-finals he tore a shoulder muscle, and that signalled the end of his racing career.

"It was a hard decision to retire him, but I think we had seen the best we were going to get from him. He was coming up for four years old, and he only had one way to go.

"He was a lovely dog to train, and I rated him as a very fine greyhound. He broke the track record three times at Nottingham, and he clocked the fastest time in the Derby heats. He was a very gutsy dog.

"But he was always unlucky, and he didn't win as much as he deserved. He reached no end of finals, but he was plagued by injury."

Larkhill Bullet, who was originally trained by Owen Mckenna, was sent back to Mckenna's Tipperary base with the Laurels at Cork in mind. But, out of the blue, tragedy struck.

"I'd had him two or three weeks, and he'd had a good few gallops, and did a nice sprint trial at Clonmel," said Mckenna. "I gave him a run at home, and when he got to the top of the gallop, he dropped instantly. It must have been a heart attack."

Charlie was devastated when he heard the news. "He was a seriously fast dog, faster than a lot of people realised because

he was forever picking up little problems which meant he didn't have that many races. When he was absolutely right, he was brilliant."

Farloe Verdict had come within a few lengths of Derby glory, and Charlie was confident that there would be plenty of wins to come. He had thoughts of trying her over six bends, but in November came the shock announcement – Droopys Hewitt was disqualified from his Derby win. He was tested in round three of the Derby, and the result was positive. According to the rules of racing, this meant that Droopys Hewitt was unplaced in the country's premier event, and runner-up Farloe Verdict was promoted to first place. On paper, this gave Charlie his fourth Greyhound Derby winner, but for him the victory was completely meaningless.

"I do rate the bitch very highly. She ran well throughout the Derby, and she was certainly good enough to win a Derby. I'm glad for Mark Bates (the owner) that she got the title. But it doesn't mean anything to me. There is no buzz to winning like that.

"I had a great chance of winning that year with three in the final, and of course I

Farloe Verdict shows them the way home in the final of the 2004 Scottish Derby.

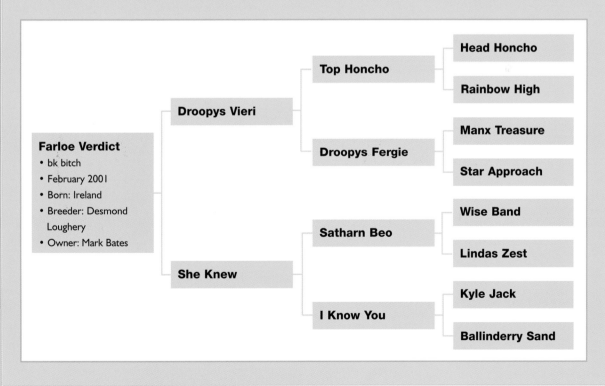

Farloe Verdict
- bk bitch
- February 2001
- Born: Ireland
- Breeder: Desmond Loughery
- Owner: Mark Bates

Droopys Vieri

Top Honcho

Head Honcho

Rainbow High

Droopys Fergie

Manx Treasure

Star Approach

She Knew

Satharn Beo

Wise Band

Lindas Zest

I Know You

Kyle Jack

Ballinderry Sand

FACT FILE

Farloe Verdict started her racing career in Ireland, and won four of her eight races. She then joined Charlie Lister's kennel, and it was not long before she notched up a couple of open race wins.

At the start of 2003, she won a heat and final at Perry Barr, and gave warning of her potential when she set a new track record of 28.80 for the 480m course. The Scottish Derby was her next challenge, and the black bitch had a first-round victory over eventual winner Micks Mystic. However, she was eliminated from the competition at the semi-final stage in a race that was disrupted by trouble.

After losing out in the final of the Hove Olympic, Charlie decided to try her in the Blue Riband at Hall Green. She reached the final without a win, but more than made up for it when breaking the track record in her 28.09 victory over the 480m course.

In the Greyhound Derby, she was very much in contention throughout the competition. She recorded wins in the first round (29.07) and in the second round (29.22). In the third round, Charlie had the misfortune of three of his dogs being drawn in the same race. Top Savings took the race, with Farloe Verdict in second place, followed by Larkhill Bullet.

Farloe Verdict maintained her runner-up spot in the quarter-finals, and again in the semis when she was beaten by Larkhill Bullet. In the £75,000 decider, she started at 12-1. She could not escape the trouble at the first bend, and finished a game runner-up behind Droopys Hewitt. Following a positive test sample from Droopys Hewitt, she was awarded the Derby crown in November 2003.

Farloe Verdict came storming back in 2004, and showed her true class when running unbeaten through the Totesport Scottish Derby. In the final, she was drawn in trap two, and never looked in any danger. She was quick away and always led to cross the winning line in a new track record of 28.79. She beat Legal Moment by 5¼ lengths.

2003 WILLIAM HILL BLUE RIBAND: FINAL RESULT

Fin.	Name	Sex	Sire	Dam	Time	Dist.	Box	Sp.	Comment
1st	Farloe Verdict	F	Droopys Vieri	She Knew	28.09		1	5-2	q aw, a ld, (**t. rec**)
2nd	Prince Toff	M	Jamella Prince	Sadlers Return	28.25	2	3	8-1	rls, clr run
3rd	Javelin King	M	Top Honcho	Lift Up	28.41	2	2	11-8f	q aw, rls – mid
4th	Greencroft Vic	M	Fancy Joe	Woodchip	28.49	1	4	6-1	mid, bmp4
5th	Baliff Champ	M	Larkhill Jo	Clacton Miss	28.67	2¼	5	6-1	mid w, crd2, bmp4
6th	Seskin Rumble	M	Smooth Rumble	Ericks Black	28.87	2½	6	25-1	s aw, w, clr run

2004 TOTESPORT SCOTTISH DERBY: FINAL RESULT

Fin.	Name	Sex	Sire	Dam	Time	Dist.	Box	Sp.	Comment
1st	Farloe Verdict	F	Droopys Vieri	She Knew	28.79		2	11-4	q aw, a ld, (**t.rec**)
2nd	Legal Moment	F	Judicial Pride	Legal Jan	29.21	5¼	3	4-1	q aw, crd1
3rd	Farloe Marathon	M	Top Honcho	Next Deal	29.23	hd	5	7-1	mod aw, b crd1
4th	Cathals Idol	M	Mustang Yank	Florida Time	29.51	3½	6	14-1	b blk1
5th	Holdyoursilence	M	Top Honcho	Misshenrietabell	30.07	7	4	33-1	mod aw, b crd1
6th	World Class	M	Come On Ranger	Queen Survivor	30.31	dist	1	11-10f	s aw, ko1

was disappointed. But there was trouble in the race, and that was an end to it. There is no glory to winning by default. Quite honestly, I am more interested in the dogs I am running in next year's Derby than to what happened months ago. I do think Farloe Verdict is a great bitch, and I hope she's remembered as that.

"We did think about racing her over six bends because she stays so strongly. She could achieve great things over the stayers trip, but she can do four-bend times, so what's the point? After all, there's not that much around for six-bend dogs."

CHAMPION TRAINER

Charlie is universally acknowledged as the country's leading trainer, but the Trainers Championship has been a prize that has always eluded him, although he has been among the top five in the ratings for the past few years.

"I am not in the business of going round the country picking off opens. I want to win the big competitions, and I only place dogs that have a very good chance of winning. I would never run dogs three or four times a week to pick up points. I'm not into points."

But in 2003, the kennel had a runaway success, and there was hardly a major final without a Lister-trained runner. Big wins were recorded by Farloe Brazil (Mr Bozz – Farloe Dingle), who scored in the Breeders Puppy Cup at Nottingham, recording 30.12 for the 500m, and the Ladbroke

Knocktoosh Queen: On a roll, with three big wins.

Gold Cup at Monmore. Starting at 9-2, the fawn dog won the 480m event in 28.12.

Knocktoosh Queen (Torbal Piper – Knocktoosh Fancy) had a tremendous season, which included three big wins. The black bitch won the Yorkshire Oaks at Sheffield, clocking 29.53 for the 500m, the National Oaks Trophy at Nottingham, and, in November, she took the Bookmakers Category Two Stakes at Sheffield. Trapping well and showing good early pace, she beat Desert Tonic by 3¼ lengths in 29.80. Moynies Cash (Joannestown Cash – Glanamoon), a promising new recruit, won the Stan James Gymcrack Puppy Championship at Hall Green.

As the wins rolled in, the points in the Trainers' Championship were notched up, and soon Charlie was sprinting away from his nearest rivals, Linda Jones and John Mullins. By the autumn Charlie was so far ahead, it was no contest.

FITTING TRIBUTE

The year ended on a high note for Charlie and the team at Mudros. Charlie received the award for Trainer of the Year, and the Greyhound Writers Association gave him a special award for Services to Greyhound Racing.

To cap it all, Charlie's assistant, Chris Akers, was voted Kennel Hand of the Year. There was a standing ovation when Charlie went up to receive his award, and he admits that it was an emotional moment.

"I know I'm not the greatest of public speakers at the best of times, but I was really choked up there. To be honest, getting that award meant a lot more to me than any trainers' title, and I really appreciate it. But it isn't just about me, we've got a really good team, with Chris, Martin (Archibold), Ian (Sutherland), and Pat – who has to put up with me on my bad days!

"I get genuine enjoyment from watching my dogs run, as long as they run well. I don't care if we finish first, fifth or tenth, provided they win the races that I think they should."

BACK IN STYLE

Charlie's decision to keep Farloe Vedict to four bends was more than justified when she showed her true class, running unbeaten to win the 2004 Totesport Scottish Derby. The black bitch was in sparkling form, and capped her triumph by setting a new track record for Shawfield's 480m. This victory was especially sweet for Charlie. He had always had a high opinion of the 2001 daughter of Droopys Vieri, and the Scottish Derby crown – won totally on her own merit – proved that she was among the best greyhounds he has trained.

"She broke the track record when winning the Blue Riband, and she's broken another track record to win a classic. She's an outstanding bitch."

THE GAME GOES ON

As always, Charlie went into the 2004 Derby with a string of hopefuls that included, Farloe Verdict, Farloe Marathon, Farloe Brazil, Knocktoosh Queen and Droopys Demagio. But there are no certainties in greyhound racing. The 2004 English Classic final was run without a Lister-trained runner. Farloe Verdict had looked in unbeatable form, but she went out in the quarter-finals when she finished lame. Droopys Demagio made his exit in the semi-finals, when the ante-post

favourite, Premier Fantasy, tragically broke a hock going into the first bend. Droopys Demagio, who had got out well, smashed into the back of the injured dog, and his Derby campaign was over.

But Charlie is not one to dwell on misfortune. There are dogs in his kennel that need feeding, training, and exercising – and there's always another race to prepare for.

The enthusiasm is as strong as ever. For Charlie, every dog – and every race – presents a new challenge. He may have spent a lifetime training greyhounds, but when a new dog comes into the kennel, he is as excited as the day he first went greyhound racing. The hopes, the dreams, the disappointments, and the occasional heartbreaks are in his blood. He is addicted to the sport, and in the same measure, he is involved with, and cares for, every greyhound in his kennel.

CHAPTER FOUR

THE RACING GREYHOUND

To compete at the top level, you need the best greyhounds. But, as many owners and trainers have discovered to their cost, it is not always the most expensive dog that turns out to be a high-class performer on the track.

"There are a lot of factors to weigh up," said Charlie. "You are looking at bloodlines in the hope that the offspring will inherit the best characteristics from their family. You are also looking at rearing, because if a dog is not correctly reared, he is never going to reach his potential. Schooling also plays a part, as this can have a long-term effect on a greyhound's style of running.

"I have had so many greyhounds over the years, and, although there are qualities you look for, there are also dogs that look

no good on paper, and then go out and surprise everyone."

BLOODLINES

When Charlie wants greyhounds, there is only one place he looks – Ireland. He said: "I would really like to see British breeding get off the ground, but at the moment, there is no competition. The Savvas have got as close as anyone. They have had some great dogs, but we will have to see if their lines continue.

"Many others have tried, but if you haven't got the right bloodlines, there is no hope. You can have a brilliant set-up, but if you haven't got the right breeding stock, you're not going to get anywhere.

"The Top On kennels have brought in American and Australian dogs to use on

British bloodlines, but I think there's a danger of losing the purity of the racing greyhound we need over here. In the USA most of the races are over 550 or 600 yards, and that requires a different type of dog."

Charlie has bred an occasional litter over the years. The most successful was when he mated the great Some Picture (1997 Scottish and English Derby winner) with Spring Rose (winner of the 1996 Grand Prix and the St. Leger), which produced Sexy Delight (2000 TV Trophy winner). However, he is a firm believer in not mixing breeding with racing.

"Breeding is a highly specialised business, and I think you need to concentrate on one thing to do it well. It also upsets the racing dogs when you are standing a dog at stud and you have visiting bitches."

REARING

Charlie has reared a few litters, but he believes that you need tailor-made facilities in order to do the job properly.

"You can rear a litter in limited space, and you may be lucky. But if you are in the business of rearing top-class greyhounds, you have to give yourself over to it. The whole place has to be planned round what is best for growing puppies. Personally, I don't believe you can combine that with a racing operation."

As far as Charlie concerned, the Irish system of rearing is unbeatable. "When you go over there, and see the freedom the dogs have, you know there is no better way. I get a lot of my greyhounds from Des Loughrey (breeder of the Farloe dogs), and he has a wonderful place. It is around 35 acres; the land is fenced, and the dogs are kept in big pens. Every day they are let out of the pens and allowed to run free. They come back to their paddocks when they are tired, or when it is time to be fed.

"The youngsters may get a few knocks, but I think that toughens them up. They are learning how to run, and how to use their bodies. The dogs thrive on it."

Rearing is a specialised business, which Charlie prefers to leave to the experts.

SCHOOLING

Charlie rarely gets involved in schooling youngsters.

"I have had a few saplings, and we have got them going on the gallop with a drag hare. We didn't have a problem with getting them ready for racing, but I have always felt that I did not have the time to do the job properly. You need a lot of patience to school a greyhound, and if you are involved with that, you are not going to give the racing dogs the time they need.

"I prefer to bring in a youngster of 14-15 months, who has had two or three trials and, maybe, one race. It is a matter of concentrating on what you do best.

"In the old days when we had different hares, it was important that dogs were schooled behind different lures, but now I would prefer the dog to be used to a Swaffham, because that is generally what he is going to come up against."

RACING PHYSIQUE

A racing greyhound is an athlete, and in order to run at speed, and negotiate bends, he has to have the physical make-up that allows him to do the job.

"I was brought up with coursing greyhounds, which tend to be bigger and stronger than track greyhounds. The average coursing dog would be 80 to 90 pounds (36-40kg) They were pacey dogs with a lot of stamina.

"I like a greyhound that is roughly around 72 to 74 pounds (33-34kg). I don't like them much bigger. It seems to me that when a big dog gets knocked off his stride, it takes him that much longer to recover.

"I like bitches of around 60 pounds (27kg). I don't like them too small, because they cannot take the knocks.

"I look for a greyhound that is well proportioned. I like to see a good, deep chest, and a long neck. The legs should be strong and straight, and I like tight, cat feet. Splayed feet are prone to injuries.

"I know there is a prejudice against blue dogs, but I have had some good blue dogs over the years. I don't care what colour a dog is, as long as he can run. But I have to admit that I do like a black dog. When you have worked on the coat, it has a beautiful sheen to it, and the dog really looks the part.

"Of course, a good-looking greyhound is not always going to be fast. I have had some funny looking dogs that have been great racers. But there is something about a good-looking dog that stands out. The dog has an air of strength and confidence, and I think that's important when it comes to racing."

RACING PHYSIQUE

Built for the job: Mickey's Bliss shows the well-proportioned physique that Charlie favours in a racing greyhound.

Droopys Natalie: A female is not as big and powerful as a male, but she needs to be strong enough to take the knocks.

TEMPERAMENT

A greyhound must have a burning desire
to chase, and he must have the courage to
go past other greyhounds, withstanding
any knocks that come his way. But it is
also important that the greyhound settles
in his kennel, eats well and is easy to
handle.

"In terms of character, I like a happy
dog. When I bring a dog out of the
kennel, I like to see him bright and outgoing. With that type of dog you can
always tell if they are a bit off-colour, or if
something is not quite right with them.
With a more moody, introverted type, it is
far harder to work out what is going on.

"I think boldness is important – you
need a brave dog who is determined to get
in front. I think sometimes problems occur
if you try to change the nature of a dog to
suit you. For example, if a dog has bone,
and he growls when you try to take it off
him, I would leave him and go back to
him later. I wouldn't reprimand him and
try to take him down a peg or two. If you
do that, you will break his spirit."

MALE V FEMALE

Charlie's kennel has been graced with
outstanding greyhounds – both male and
female – but he believes a male is

*Charlie pictured with Knocktoosh Queen (left)
and El Ronan (right). A top-class male is more
likely to have the edge on a female – but
bitches can show great consistency when they
hit form.*

potentially a superior performer on the
track.

"I am always interested in a fast bitch,
but, at the highest level, you are more
likely to hit the jackpot with a dog. A male
is bigger and stronger than a female, and
so a good dog is always going to beat a
good bitch. You can have a very fast bitch,
but she is always going to come off worse
if there is trouble."

Often bitches will come into their own
in stayers races. "A bitch will often carry
on racing for longer than a male,

particularly if she goes over the stayers' distance. I have found that a good bitch can be very consistent when she hits form. Knocktoosh Queen (winner of the Yorkshire Oaks and National Oaks in 2003) is a good example of that. She always gives her best, and she is nearly always in contention."

IN-SEASON BITCHES

Obviously, a trainer has to plan around a bitch's seasonal cycle. This can be a frustrating time for trainers and owners, but Charlie has found one benefit from keeping close tabs on a bitch's seasonal dates. "When a season is due, a bitch can give you a flying run."

The NGRC allows a bitch to return to the track three weeks after her season has finished, but Charlie will not allow his bitches to do this. He is a firm believer in allowing a bitch a full 12 weeks off when she is in season.

"I don't think it is right to expect a bitch to perform as an athlete when she is still going through hormonal changes. I don't see how you can expect her to give her best – and I have certainly never seen a bitch run well when she is just out of season.

"The problem is that there is such a high demand for dogs, most tracks cannot get by if they lose their bitches off the racing strength for that amount of time. For example, Nottingham race three times a week, plus hold BAGS meetings, which means they are racing five or six times a week. You need an awful lot of dogs to keep pace with those demands."

He is also against the suppression of seasons. "There are some owners who insist on it, particularly if you have a bitch that comes in season every six months. But I don't like doing it – in my view, it's messing with nature.

"At about 10 weeks out of season, I would give the bitch a few gallops, and would trial her at 12 weeks. The bitch will generally need a few races to get back to top form – which usually happen at around 18 to 20 weeks."

TALENT SPOTTING

If you want the best dogs, you need to get in early before the rest of the world has spotted a greyhound's potential.

"I have a number of scouts in Ireland, who are on the look-out for good dogs. They go to the schooling tracks and the racetracks and see what looks promising. When they find something that sounds interesting, I go over and watch the dog run."

Charlie can generally tell if a dog has potential after watching a single trial.

"I am looking for a dog with good early pace who will get 500m – that is essential if you want to compete at the top level. I have had some great sprinters, and some great stayers in my kennel, but at the outset, you are looking for a classic middle-distance dog.

"There are some dogs who change as their career progresses. A dog may start off over four bends, and then develop into a stayer."

Charlie describes his ideal greyhound as one who pops out of the traps and sticks to the rails.

"It stands to reason that a railer does not need to cover so much ground as a wide runner. You often see dogs go out so wide that they give themselves a real job to get in front. A railer who gets out in front is far less likely to be bumped."

It is during schooling that a dog shows a preference for the rails or for the outside, and, according to Charlie, there is nothing you can do to change his style of running.

"I have had dogs that were true middle runners, but the vast majority favour either the inside or the outside. I think it is often the dogs that are schooled to an inside hare that end up as railers. Occasionally you get a dog who seems to be born with tactical skills, and can run from almost any box. Burberry Boy (winner of the East Anglian Derby in 2003) could make the best of any box he was put in."

Charlie can generally assess a greyhound's potential after watching a single trial.

A three-dog trial will show a dog's pace, and whether he has the guts to go by.

Early pace is an essential ingredient, but, at the top level, it is just as important to have a dog that has the stamina to stay for 500m.

"I have had dogs with bags of early, but they struggle to get 460m. That can be just as frustrating as the dog who lacks early pace.

"I have always liked stayers. To my mind, a stayer is always in with a chance, as there is more time to get out of trouble. Staying dogs also tend to carry on racing for longer."

HURDLERS

When you look at Charlie's long list of winners, there is a notable absence of hurdlers. "I have to admit that I have never been keen on hurdlers, and I have never trained a dog over the jumps," he said.

"The old cure for a dodgy dog was to put him over hurdles. If a dog was not quite genuine, the jumps gave him something to think about. I have always wanted to train the best dogs, so I wasn't interested in hurdle racing.

"These days it has changed, and there are some dogs that are schooled to go over hurdles right from the start. A hurdle race can look really spectacular, but you can still tell that some of the dogs are not 100 per cent genuine – and that can make a farce out of a race."

BUYING GREYHOUNDS

Charlie has no shortage of owners who want to place greyhounds with him, and many give him the task of finding the right dog.

"When someone rings up and says they want a dog, I tell them it could take months before we find the right one. After all, if they are spending £20,000 or more to get a top dog, I don't want to make a mistake. In fact, if you want a Derby contender, it could cost as much as £50,000. For most owners, money is not the object. They want to own a top dog that is capable of winning the major prizes.

"Business is booming in Ireland, and I blame the agents for bumping up the prices. There is good money to be made, and everyone wants to get in on the act. It makes buying greyhounds a nightmare.

"I like to see a dog run in a three-dog trial, and then I can assess pace, and see if a dog has guts and doesn't chicken out. I like to see a dog passing other dogs.

"One of the hardest aspects is comparing times on different schooling tracks, and working out how they are affected by the going. I always take my stopwatch with me, so I can make my own calculations.

"After watching the dog run, I talk to the owner and see if they are interested. The problem is that dogs are expensive, and even though you see something you like, there is no guarantee that the dog is going to go on and win big races.

"Over the years we have had some expensive failures. I remember Frank Kearney paid £13,000 for a dog and it never won a race. It can be very awkward, but there is only so much you can do to get a dog running."

Charlie steers clear of having a personal stake in any of the dogs in his kennel.

"When Val was alive, we used to own a number of dogs in her name – but I don't do that kind of thing any more. I get offered dogs all the time, but there is no sense in getting financially involved. It just wouldn't be profitable."

NEW RECRUITS

When a new dog comes into the kennel, Charlie will give him a month or so to settle before he tries to do anything with him.

"I like the dog to adjust to his new home before I ask anything of him. I would then give him a couple of gallops at home, and then move on to trials."

At this stage, Charlie takes the dog to a number of different tracks.

"I like youngsters to run at least three different tracks so they get an idea of different circuits, and I can judge them properly. It helps to build up a picture of how the dog runs, and it gets the dog accustomed to different circuits. If you stick to one track, the dog will get used to it, and may decide he doesn't want to run away from home.

"I once had a litter of pups when I was attached to Nottingham. They were unbeaten at Nottingham, but, when I took them to another track, they didn't want to know. As soon as we switched back to Nottingham, they started running again."

RETIRED DOGS

One of the hardest aspects of owning and training greyhounds is finding a future for a dog when his racing career is over.

"I am lucky because most of my owners care about their dogs. Of course, they like to have a bet, but they are concerned about the dogs' welfare. There are not many who come to see the dogs in the kennels, but that is because I live a long way from most of them. But they will take an interest in the dog and work out what to do when it is time to retire him.

"I have managed to find homes for quite a few dogs locally, and it's really nice to see them settled in a new home. Greyhounds do make lovely pets.

"Over the years, I have had a few dogs that have been left in the kennel, which is a shame when the dog has done well for his

owners on the track. But, to my mind, a dog does not cost a lot to feed, and so he will always have a home. I would never have a dog put down because he had reached the end of his racing career.

"We have kept a lot of old dogs down the years, and many are buried in the garden – their graves are marked with flowers."

Charlie is not a man to show his emotions easily, but he is a big softie when it comes to his dogs.

One of the hardest decisions he had to make was when Superior Champ (winner of the 1978 Silver Salver and 1980 Northern Sprint Championship) started to fail in health.

"Jack, as we called him, was a marvellous old dog, but, when he was 15, his back legs went. I knew what I should do, and I called out the vet. I went to get Jack out of his kennel, and he just looked up at me, and I couldn't go through with it.

"A week or so later, we went through the whole thing again, and I still couldn't go through with it. In the end, I had to go to Ireland, and Val arranged for the vet to come while I was away. We buried him in the garden."

CHAPTER FIVE

LIFE AT MUDROS

Charlie's house and kennels occupy a five-acre site in the small village of South Clifton, near Newark in Nottinghamshire. Charlie has lived there for the last 12 years, and, during that time, he has completely rebuilt the house, and developed the kennels.

"There used to be a two-bedroom bungalow on the site, and when we drove past, my wife, Val, always used to say what a pretty place it was. She always said she would like to live there. One day, I was driving past, and I saw a 'For Sale' sign being put up. I got on to the estate agent straight away and bought it. We did the house up over a number of years, and we moved in three years before Val died."

The house is spacious and comfortable, and, as you would expect, the walls are lined with paintings and photographs of Charlie's top dogs. There are trophies on every surface, and there are more packed in boxes, along with presentation racing jackets.

"We simply don't have the room to display everything. Of course, the owners have quite a few of the trophies and the racing jackets, but we are still running out of space."

Despite his many victories, Charlie is as hungry as ever to win the big races.

"I love to see my dogs run, and I love to see them win. I can honestly say that I enjoy watching the dogs run as much now as the day I started."

Some trainers are meticulous about recording their dogs' successes, but although Charlie cares passionately about every competition his dogs enter, he does

The trophy room at Mudros: Charlie has run out of room to display all his trophies...

not spend time reflecting on past glories.

"If you were to ask me how many races my dogs had won over the years, I wouldn't have a clue. If we have a big win, people say: 'I bet you were celebrating for a week afterwards'. But the next morning we just carry on the same as always. We've got dogs to feed, and we have races to get ready for. We're too busy to think about what happened the night before. That is not to say that I don't enjoy winning. It is what keeps all of us going."

Charlie has a number of retired greyhounds in his kennels, but the Jack Russells, Twiggy and Tania, rule in the house.

"We have always kept Jack Russells – I love them because they have so much character," said Charlie. But it is Joel, the African Grey Parrot, that is the star turn.

"Des Loughrey, who breeds the Farloe dogs in Ireland, has a parrot, and I was really taken with him. Des taught him to say 'Charlie Lister' so he could greet me when I went there. Pat and I decided we had to have one.

"Joel is a fantastic talker. He picks up words and phrases so quickly. He mimics me and Pat, and he can do an exact imitation of the phone ringing. We have two lines, with different rings, and he can do them both perfectly.

"The only trouble is, he listens to me when I'm on the phone. I can get a bit irate when something's gone wrong, and, the next thing you know, he's copying my bad language!"

THE STAFF

The Lister kennel is manned by a team of five. As well as Charlie and his partner, Pat Cartledge, there is assistant trainer Chris Akers, and kennel hands Ian Sutherland and Martin Archibold. The three kennel staff live on site, so they can cope with the late nights and early mornings that the job demands.

"You get some lads thinking that they can work from 9am to 4pm, and then they can go racing. But the job is not like that. I'm lucky that I have good staff who are prepared to put in the hours.

"My present staff are the best I've ever had. They are reliable, and they understand the dogs. Some kennel hands only stay for a matter of months, but my staff have all been with me for a long stretch."

Charlie is tough, but fair, and although he looks after his staff, he expects a lot from them. Punctuality is a particular bugbear.

"When I had the timber yard, I always arrived first so I would be there when the staff arrived. It showed them that if the boss was on time, they had to be, too."

The Mudros team: Pictured (left to right) Martin Archibold, Chris Akers (assistant trainer), and Ian Sutherland.

Since his stroke in January 2002, Charlie takes life a little easier – staying in bed until 7.30am before going down to the kennels, regardless of the time he arrived home from racing the night before.

"I am used to working hard, and you get used to the late nights. It might be 1.30 or 2am before we get home from some tracks, and then we still have the dogs to feed. The other night I had to poultice a dog's toe when we got back in the early hours. I didn't want to leave it until the morning."

If one of the lads has returned late home from racing, he will be allowed a lie-in the following morning. But that will not do for Charlie.

"I like to be there to get the dogs out and to give them breakfast."

Charlie keeps a very close eye on how the kennels are run, but he is not frightened to delegate.

"I trust my staff to do a lot of the work in the kennels. I like to show someone how to do a job, and then I expect them to catch on. I don't mind showing them a couple or three times, but I can't stand having someone who keeps on asking no matter how many times you've shown them what to do."

DELEGATING JOBS

Charlie has taught the kennel staff his methods of grooming and massage, and they can treat minor injuries. They also divide up the exercise requirements with some road walking while others take dogs to the gallop.

"I like to share out the work so that everyone has a bit of variety in what they do. We take it in turns as to who goes racing, or who takes dogs to trials. We always leave two people behind so that the dogs can be let out in the evening, and then be settled for the night.

"A number of people who have worked for me have gone on to take out their own training licence, and a few have been quite successful. I like to see people having the chance to get on.

"Michael Harris was with me for four years, and he is now training at Monmore. His father got him some kennels, and when he told me he was leaving, he said he wouldn't go until I found a replacement. After six weeks, I told him he had to go. He had to get going on his own. But he was such a good worker, he didn't want to leave me in the lurch."

One thing Charlie cannot stand is seeing a trainer hog the limelight. "You see some trainers who let the kennel hand parade a dog, put him in the traps, and then catch him after the race. But if the dog wins a big race, the trainer suddenly appears and takes the dog off the kennel hand so that he can be there for the interviews and the photographs. I don't believe in doing that. I think everyone should get a taste of success."

Although jobs are shared in the kennels, Charlie likes to stick to a routine at the track. "If one of the lads travels with a greyhound and looks after him at the track, I try to keep that going in every round of the competition, including the final. It gives the greyhound a sense of consistency, and the lads like to be involved all the way through."

There are odd occasions when Charlie will parade a dog and put him in the traps. For example, if he has more than one dog in a race. "Mostly, I leave that side of things to the lads. I like to be in a good position to see the race, and it's a side of the work the lads enjoy.

"I don't think the tracks treat kennel staff at all well, and I try to do my best to change that. It wouldn't hurt if they provided a meal for the kennel hands, rather than leaving them to buy a burger and chips at an inflated price from the track.

"Some tracks are better than others. In Ireland, you get treated really well. I remember going to Tralee, and being greeted by one of the track staff, and being shown where I could get a meal. The big tracks make so much money. I reckon they could afford to make life a bit easier for the kennel staff."

DAILY ROUTINE

Establishing an efficient routine is essential when you are looking after a kennel of around 35 greyhounds, each with his own special needs. There are dogs that are competing, dogs being prepared for big competitions, dogs being rested, bitches in season, dogs being treated for injuries, plus a few oldies who still need regular care.

Over the years, Charlie has established a routine that works well for the dogs and for the staff.

- **6.30-7am:** The dogs are let out in turn, and have a short spell in the outside paddocks. If the weather is poor, the covered paddocks are used (see page 89). While the dogs are outside, the kennels are cleaned and disinfected, and the bedding is topped up (see page 87).
- **8-8.30am:** Breakfast is fed to all dogs (see page 93).
- **9am:** The dogs are turned out. Kennel cleaning is completed, plus the routine cleaning of the corridors, feed room, and paddocks. When required, a member of staff will be delegated to take a greyhound to the vet (who is based in Milton Keynes) or a dog may need to be taken for a trial.
- **10am:** Grooming and massage. Dogs that have raced the night before are

checked (see page 107). Priority for massage is given to dogs that are racing that night, but all dogs are groomed on a daily basis (see page 101).
- **11am-1pm:** Exercise. This may entail road walking or galloping. Every couple of weeks, a batch of dogs may be taken swimming (see page 115).
- **Midday:** Dogs are turned out (see page 89). Feeds are made up. This includes main meals and pre-race meals. Main meals for racing dogs will be put to one side to be fed last thing at night.
- **2.30pm:** The main meal is fed to all dogs that are not racing. A pre-race meal is fed to competitors (see page 98).
- **3pm:** Dogs are turned out. Dogs leave for racing. When possible, trials are arranged before racing to avoid extra journeys to the tracks. Veterinary treatments are given to injured dogs (see Chapter 14).
- **6-7pm:** Dogs are turned out and then settled for the night. This may be later (8-9pm) in the summer. Two members of staff always stay behind on race nights to look after the dogs in kennels.
- **Midnight (or later):** Return from racing. Greyhounds are fed their main meal. Any urgent treatment is carried out before settling the dogs for the night.

CHAPTER SIX

THE KENNELS

Charlie Lister started racing greyhounds as a hobby, just keeping a few dogs at home. When he turned professional and worked as a contract trainer, he had as many as 50 greyhounds at a time, but now he prefers to keep the numbers down. He currently has around 35 to 40 greyhounds in his care.

"Ideally, I would keep 30 to 35 greyhounds, but the numbers do creep up a bit. I am always being asked to take on dogs, but I don't want to take on any more than I can do properly. There are five of us working here, and that works out at six or seven dogs per person. With that ratio, we know our dogs, and we are quick to spot if anything is wrong.

"If a trainer has 200 dogs in his kennel, it is impossible to know what is going on with every dog. That's how things go wrong. Even fundamental things, like spotting an injury, can be missed. We can cope with the number we have, and I can make a living out of it. If you let the numbers drop to 20 to 25 dogs, you are beginning to struggle. You have to spread the wages and the expenses around a reasonable number of dogs in order to make it pay."

When Charlie first moved to Mudros, there were some old buildings, which he has replaced with purpose-built kennels and a feed room. The feed room also doubles up as a grooming area, and it has scales for weighing the dogs.

"The kennels are nothing out of the ordinary. I didn't go for anything fancy, but the dogs have plenty of room, and they are always comfortable."

There are two blocks of kennels – one block is for racers, the other is for bitches in season, resting dogs, and retired dogs. The buildings are made of breeze blocks.

"I would always choose breeze blocks ahead of timber," said Charlie. "You get much better insulation against the weather, so you can keep out the draughts. You can always have the buildings rendered and painted if you want to make them more attractive."

The kennels are lined on one side, with a corridor running alongside them. The floor is made of concrete, and it slopes slightly downwards from the kennels so that water can drain into a gully that runs the length of the corridor. Ventilation vents are fitted into the walls at the back of each kennel, and there are windows that run the full length of the kennel block. Depending on the weather, the windows are opened to let in the fresh air.

"I think it is very important to have fresh air circulating," said Charlie. "The spread of germs is one of the biggest problems you have when you kennel dogs together, and so you need to keep the kennels scrupulously clean, and allow as much fresh air as possible."

The kennel blocks are fitted with central heating. In the winter, the temperature is kept at around 10 degrees Centigrade (50F). "The aim is to take the chill off; we don't want the kennels to be too warm. But the dogs are comfortable, and don't need to wear coats in the kennels."

A bucket of water is provided in every kennel, and is changed daily. If necessary, the bucket is chained to the wall to prevent water spills.

VITAL STATISTICS

- A single kennel (for one greyhound) measures eight feet (2.5m) in length, and is six feet (1.9m) wide.
- A double kennel (for one male and one female greyhound) measures eight feet (2.5m) in length, and is ten feet (3.1m) wide.

The door to each kennel is made of galvanised steel, and is secured with a sliding bolt. Inside each kennel, there is a raised bed, which is between 18 inches and two feet off the ground. The bed boards are made of plywood, and the frames are wooden, with an aluminium strip across the front to stop dogs chewing.

In a single kennel, the bed measures the full width of the kennel, and from the back

CHARLIE'S KENNELS

The kennels are lined on one side, with a corridor running alongside.

A single bed measures 8 ft in length, and is 6 ft wide.

The door to each kennel is made of galvanised steel, and secured with a sliding bolt.

A lowered bed is used for injured dogs.

Every greyhound is given a deep, comfortable bed, which is topped up regularly.

wall, it comes out around four feet (1.2m). In a double kennel, the bed is the same depth and around 10 feet (3.1m) wide.

"A raised bed is essential. The dog is kept out of draughts, and you can keep the bedding from spilling on to the floor. In most cases, a dog won't foul his bed, and so the sleeping area always stays clean and dry."

BED WETTERS

There are greyhounds that refuse to be clean in the kennel, and persistently wet their bedding. Charlie has a cunning solution for this problem.

"We put a ledge above the bed which prevents the dog from standing when he is on his bed. He has plenty of space to stand in front of his bed, but he has to lie down when he is on his sleeping area. Nine times out of ten, this stops the greyhound spending on his bed."

INJURED DOGS

There are also a couple of kennels with a lowered bed, which are used for greyhounds who are injured.

"If you have an injured dog, the last thing you want is to have him jumping on and off his bed all day, so we use a kennel with a bed just above ground level when a dog is recuperating."

BEDDING

Charlie remembers the time when straw was widely used for bedding. "It made a comfortable bed, but it was very labour intensive. It was also very dusty, which didn't suit some greyhounds."

He now uses shredded-paper bedding, alternating between two types depending on the season. In the warm summer months, he uses brown shredded paper. The paper is slightly coated, which helps to keep the bed dry and springy. "I have found that this type of bedding does not dry the coat out too much," he said.

When it is colder, he changes over to a bedding that is made of shredded J-cloths. "It makes a very good bed in the winter. It is warm, and it is completely dust-free. As we have central heating, I do not have to worry too much about keeping the greyhounds warm – none of them wear kennel coats – but they do need a nice bed."

Charlie does not believe in economising on bedding. He likes the beds to be laid deep so there is no chance of a greyhound lying directly on the bed boards. "You need a good depth of bed, and then you can shake it up when you clean out the kennel."

The other advantage is that both types

of bedding can be burnt, and Charlie has an incinerator to do this. If waste cannot be burnt in the incinerator, it is put into a skip, which is emptied at regular intervals.

"I have tried different types of bedding, including polythene, but I have found that using the two different types works best. It is important to keep the bed topped up with fresh bedding. When the dogs go out first thing in the morning, we sweep up the bedding that has fallen on the floor, and top up the bed. Every week we take out the entire bed, and disinfect the kennel. Obviously, there are some dogs who are messy in their kennels, and we would have to clean them out more frequently."

CLEANLINESS IS NEXT TO...

Hygiene is the watchword in the Mudros kennel, and the kennels and runs are kept scrupulously clean.

The kennels are cleaned out daily; the floor space is disinfected, and the corridors are scrubbed clean. The grooming area and feed room are also immaculate.

According to Pat Cartledge, the Mudros kennel was known in the neighbourhood for its smell of Jeyes Fluid.

"I reckon you could smell Jeyes Fluid if you drove past!" she said.

Jeyes fluid is still a popular choice, but a slightly scented disinfectant is also used to sweeten the overwhelming smell of cleanliness.

"If you get sickness in a kennel, it soon spreads," said Charlie. "You have to work overtime at keeping the place clean and disinfected."

KENNEL COMPANIONS

Charlie treats every greyhound in his kennel as an individual and tries to provide for all the dogs' specific needs. Some greyhounds prefer to be kennelled alone, others like to have company.

"If I kennel two greyhounds together, it is always a dog and a bitch. It is too dangerous to kennel two males together. If they start a fight, it can be a hell of a job to stop it. It is pretty much the same with two bitches. They are just as likely to fight."

"Kennelling in pairs works if you have a young dog who finds it hard to settle. If you put him in with a mature bitch, she will calm him down."

When the dogs are first put in the kennel together, they are both muzzled. "We keep the muzzles on for a few days until we are sure there is not going to be any trouble. After that, we leave them off."

Whenever possible, Charlie likes to keep the dogs unmuzzled. "I wouldn't like something round my face all day, and I can't think a dog does either. That's just my opinion – other people might disagree.

"We do find that dogs that are kennelled together can snap at each other, even if they get on well. For instance, if one dog jumps on the bed and lands on the other dog, it might cause trouble, so you do have to be careful.

"However, there are definitely some dogs that run better if they have company, and so it's a matter of finding a pair that will get on well together."

BEST MATES

"I was once offered a Jack Russell pup, and it looked so pretty sitting in this box, I couldn't resist it. This little pup became great friends with Swift Band (East Anglian Derby winner, 1981). They used to play together, and Swift Band was ever so gentle – he used to close his mouth over the little dog, but he would never have dreamt of harming him."

TURNOUT

Any dog that is confined to a kennel for long periods becomes bored and unhappy. If the dog does not have the opportunity

Some dogs will settle better if they have company.

to relieve himself at regular intervals, this adds to his discomfort.

The daily routine at Mudros is geared to giving the greyhounds as much regular turnout as possible. There are 20 grass paddocks, which each measure around 50 feet (15m) square. In addition there are three covered indoor paddocks, which measure approximately 20 feet (6m) by 25 feet (8m), which are used in bad weather. Overhanging trees provide natural shade in most of the outside paddocks, but, as the dogs are not kept out for long periods, there is no need to provide additional shelter. The paddocks have metal fencing, fitted to concrete posts, and the minimum height is 6 feet 6 inches (2m).

DAILY TURNOUT

Regular turnout in the outside paddocks is an essential part of kennel routine.

Covered indoor paddocks are used in bad weather.

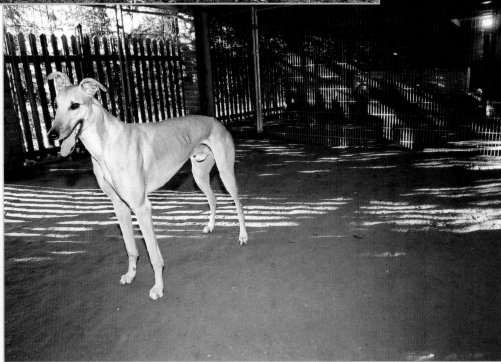

"I wouldn't dare go for fencing any lower than that. I had a bitch called Slideaway Snoopy who got over the fence a couple of times. She was a nice bitch, and belonged to Bert Ullyett, owner of Chesterfield Stadium. She won the Sunderland Oaks and the Peterborough Cesarewitch – and she certainly had a good spring in her to clear a six-foot fence!"

The rule is: one dog to a paddock, and the dogs are rotated so that they are all let out five or six times during the course of a day. The last job of the day is to turn out the dogs between 6pm and 7pm, before shutting them in for the night. In hot weather, the dogs may be let out as late as 9pm, so that they can take advantage of the cooler evening temperatures.

"The dogs are not out for long – maybe 10 or 15 minutes – but it gives them the chance to stretch their legs, to empty, and to look at what is going on around them. No dog will thrive if he is cooped up all day."

Obviously, this system of turnout is very labour intensive, but Charlie sees it as absolutely essential.

"In the big kennels, where they have up to 200 dogs, it is impossible to give that much turnout, and I think it is a major drawback. I like my dogs to be happy and comfortable. There are some dogs who really don't like to foul the kennel, and they will go for hours until they have the opportunity to go out. I don't think that is good for a dog. Rapid Ranger (dual English Derby winner) was like that. He would rather burst than wet in his kennel. I think a dog can damage his kidneys if he not allowed to relieve himself when he wants to, and that is why I insist on so much turnout in my kennel."

The turnout paddocks need to be kept scrupulously clean, and picking up in the paddocks is a regular job for the staff.

"We rest paddocks every so often to give the grass a chance to recover. I'm amazed at how well it grows back after a break."

SAFETY FIRST

Whenever a greyhound is taken out to a paddock, or when he is going from the kennel to be groomed or weighed, a collar and lead is always used.

"There are some trainers who let the dogs run along the corridor if it is enclosed, but I would never allow that. We have valuable dogs here, and accidents can happen all too easily. I would rather be cautious than risk a dog getting injured."

FEEDING TIME

The dogs are fed in their kennels. If two

dogs are kennelled together, one of the kennel staff will supervise them while they are feeding. Generally, one dog will be fed on the bed, and the other will be fed on the floor. The dogs are never left alone when they are feeding.

PLAY IT AGAIN

Each block of kennels has a radio, which is kept turned on during the day.

"I think it helps the dogs to settle and stops them barking. It is also useful if you want to mask noises.

"For example, Spring Rose (winner of the 1996 Grand Prix and St. Leger), is terrified of thunder. If we turn up the radio full blast, she can't hear the thunder so she doesn't get agitated. We do the same when there's a clay pigeon shoot nearby."

DESTRUCTIVE DOGS

There are some greyhounds who are intent on destroying their kennel, no matter how comfortable it is.

"We keep wood in the kennel down to a minimum. We have aluminium strips protecting the bed, and the doors are made of metal. But sometimes you will get a dog who is very determined.

"It is more likely to happen when a greyhound is not racing, so he has nothing to keep his mind occupied. Sometimes a dog can be frightened, and that can lead to destructive behaviour. Spring Rose can literally rip her kennel to pieces if she gets alarmed."

A muzzle will obviously limit the damage a greyhound can do, and Charlie also finds that the radio has a calming influence.

CHAPTER SEVEN

FEEDING RACING GREYHOUNDS

Charlie Lister looks after the country's top canine athletes, and, as you would expect, diet is a matter of the utmost importance.

"You have got to keep the dogs fit and well, and in order for them to give their best, they must be fed the best," he said.

Brought up in the old school of greyhound training, Charlie is a traditionalist when it comes to feeding. He has adapted his methods over the years, but he remains a firm believer in providing top-quality fresh food.

TO START THE DAY

Breakfast is given to all the dogs in the kennel, regardless of whether they are racing or not. This consists of a scoop of cereal, which is usually a mixture of

Breakfast: Charlie is a great believer in adding honey to the cereal feed.

cornflakes and Weetabix, a raw egg, and warm milk, which is made up from a powdered formula.

"I add a spoonful of honey to the breakfast meal, as I think it is good for energy," said Charlie. "I would also add glucose for dogs that are racing that day." The only dogs that are not given breakfast are those that are trialling in the morning. They are fed a small pre-race meal (see page 98).

Charlie makes a meat stew to his own tried-and-trusted recipe.

MAIN MEAL

The main meal of the day is fed early afternoon, at around 2.30pm. This means that dogs that are racing can be fed at the same time as non-racers. Like the triallists, they receive a small pre-race meal (see page 98).

"If the racing dogs are not fed at the same time, they will fret and will not settle. They are used to being fed at the same time each day, and it is important to keep them in a routine – even if they are not being given a main meal."

Thinking of what will suit the dog, rather than what is most convenient, is typical of the way Charlie looks after his greyhounds, and is one of the reasons why he is so successful. His top priority is to provide an environment where the dogs will thrive. The main meal consists of a scoop of Red Mills or Wafcol complete feed. Charlie changes between the two brands in order to provide variety. The complete food, plus fresh brown bread is soaked thoroughly in Charlie's meat stew.

"I keep a meat stew on the go all the time. It is made with a meat stock, and I add carrots, cabbage and pasta."

If a dog has a tendency to cramp in races, he will add canned tomatoes, which he has found to be a very effective way of treating the problem.

"It is way of giving more Vitamin C, which the dogs can absorb easily."

Meat is supplied from the local slaughterhouse and it will usually be horse or cattle meat.

"The meat is good quality, but I think it is okay if there is a reasonable level of fat. I think fat helps to keep overall condition and it certainly helps coat condition. In fact, if a dog has a very dry coat, I would add some suet to the main meal."

Generally, a dog will be given one pound of meat, and a bitch around 12 ounces. If a greyhound is resting or injured, the meat content will be cut to around eight ounces.

RAW OR COOKED MEAT?

The decision on whether to feed raw or cooked meat, or the proportion of raw meat to cooked meat that is fed, depends on a greyhound's individual workload.

"If a dog is resting, or is not doing very much, I cook the meat. However, I don't like to overcook it, or you lose all the goodness.

"For dogs that are racing, I feed a proportion of raw meat. I would probably feed half the ration of meat cooked, and half raw. I find raw meat gives the dogs that little bit extra. If a dog is going

Racing dogs will be fed a proportion of raw meat.

through the rounds of a major competition, I may increase the amount of raw meat. It depends on what is right for the individual dog."

Getting to know the individual, and working out what suits a particular dog, lies at the heart of Charlie's training system. He is not content to stick with a regime simply because it suits most dogs – it must be tailored to the individual.

Charlie is more than ready to share his knowledge and his experience of looking after greyhounds, but when it comes to it, he relies on his own evaluation of a dog. He then makes decisions based on his own experience, and his understanding of a what that particular dog needs.

MEASURE FOR MEASURE

Every dog has his own bowl, labelled with his kennel name. Every part of the diet is weighed, and is adjusted according to the needs of that particular dog.

"Some dogs are very good doers, and they keep the weight on without any effort. Other dogs you have to feed up.

"I remember Yellow Cowboy (winner of an Invitation Stakes at Crayford). He was a terrible eater. When he arrived here, he wouldn't take a bite of food. I tried him on everything to tempt his appetite, But he turned up his nose at it all, even raw steak.

"We have a tripe factory nearby, so I got some green tripe and tried him on that. It did the trick. He liked the tripe and that got him eating again. After that, he was all right – although he was a dog that needed big feeds to keep the weight on."

Every greyhound in the kennel has his own personalised feed bowl.

FADDY FEEDERS

Occasionally a greyhound will become picky about his food, and will start to leave some of his rations.

"Farloe Brazil (winner of the 2003 Ladbrokes Gold Cup) got into the habit of eating half his food, and then leaving the rest. To begin with, we left the bowl in his kennel overnight so that he could finish it. However, I then decided to fetch the bowl out after 10 minutes or so, when he had stopped eating. After Charlie had removed Farloe Brazil's bowl a few times, the problem seemed to be resolved:

"He soon leant to eat all his meal up. It is not a good idea to let a dog get too fussy. If he is hungry, he will eat."

RACING STRESS

There are greyhounds that lose weight in races, due to the stress and exertion of competing.

"These are the dogs you have to watch out for, as condition can deteriorate very quickly," said Charlie.

If a dog struggles to maintain his weight, Charlie increases the overall quantity of food, rather than giving an extra meal.

"I find that the pasta in the stew is a good way of keeping on the weight."

GOOD DOERS

Some greyhounds seem to exist on thin air, and it is all too easy to overfeed this type of dog.

"Knockaun Joker, a marathon bitch, hardly needed to eat anything. She was not a big bitch, but I was always amazed by how little she needed. I would look at her food and think: 'How can you race on that?' But she could. She was just one of the types that could make good use of her food."

WEIGHED IN

It is vital that the weight of racing greyhounds does not fluctuate, and so not only is the food weighed at every meal, the dogs are weighed daily too.

"We find that by weighing the food, we can keep weight pretty consistent. You might think you are giving the correct quantity just by measuring with your eye, or by giving roughly a scoopful or a handful, but that is not accurate enough.

"We feed the main meal wet, but it is not sloppy in consistency. If you feed too wet, it puts too much of a belly on a dog.

You need to keep a racing dog well covered, but lean."

SUPPLEMENTS

Regular supplements of Vitamin C are given, and a multi-vitamin supplement, such as SA37, is also added to the main meal.

"There are so many supplements available these days, you can spend a fortune. Personally, I think that if you are feeding a well-balanced diet, most of them are a waste of money. I think you should guard against over-supplementing."

There is also the very real danger of introducing something that may show up as an illegal substance when a dog gives a urine sample.

Every feed is weighed out individually.

Charlie is cautious in his use of supplements.

"You have to be so careful these days. We have to double-check everything we feed, and every medicine that we give. The kennel hands know how important this is, and that is why we monitor every meal that we feed."

Charlie remembers all too well the stewards' inquiry relating to Grand Prix winner Spring Rose.

"In those days, I used to give my dogs a drink of tea before we went racing. It was something I had always done, and I didn't think anything of it.

"We stopped on the way to Walthamstow to give the bitch a chance to empty, but she was a nervous type, and she wouldn't do anything because of the noise of the traffic. We decided to wait until we got to Walthamstow, but they had a big band playing, and the sound of all the drums and everything put her off, and she still wouldn't go.

"At that time, all racing greyhounds had to give a routine sample, and so we had to keep on trying. It was 10.20 that night before she eventually gave a sample."

The sample was tested, and very slight traces of caffeine were found. Charlie was fined £1,000.

"I was absolutely gutted. I didn't realise I was doing anything wrong, and the vet said it was probably because the bitch had held her water for so long, that traces of caffeine were found.

"Of course, I realise now that I shouldn't have given the tea, but the stewards' inquiry is so degrading – it makes you feel like a criminal. I understand that the rules must be strict, but I don't think trainers who have a reputation for being straight should be treated like that."

PRE-RACE MEAL

If a dog is racing, a special pre-race meal is prepared. This consists of cereal, honey, and glucose plus some raw meat. This may be no more than a couple of ounces; it is just enough to give a taste of meat.

"We feed the pre-race meal at around 2.30pm, and this gives sufficient nourishment to last the dog until he is ready to race," said Charlie.

AFTER RACING

When a greyhound comes off the track, he is given a drink of water with added electrolytes, which help to replace body salts and other minerals. On the way home, particularly if it is a long journey, the racers are given a drink of milk. When they return to the kennels, they are fed their regular main meal ration.

AN ATHLETE'S DIET

Every trainer has his own opinions on diet and nutrition, and, for some trainers with large kennels, convenience also plays a part. But, on the whole, Charlie sticks to his tried-and-trusted methods.

"Everyone has got their own way of doing things, and I respect that. But I have been training greyhounds a long time, and I wouldn't change something if it was working for me. I wouldn't change the diet I was feeding just because a new product came on the market, making all sorts of claims. I know the diet I feed works for my greyhounds. But equally, I like to keep myself open to new ideas, and

The skilled trainer has confidence in his methods, and does not need to chop and change diets.

new ways of doing things.

"I have come to rely on the traditional method of feeding because I think it is the best way of keeping a dog fit and healthy over an extended period of time. I am not interested in hyping up a dog for one race. You might boost performance in the short term, but a dog will soon get burnt out.

"I take the long view. I want my dogs to race at the top level for as long as they possibly can. Many of our dogs have carried on racing at the top until four years old and beyond, and I think that has a lot to do with diet.

"In a big kennel, there is probably not enough time to pay so much attention to feeding. It is obviously so much quicker and easier to feed a complete diet. But I don't think the dogs do so well on it. I know I wouldn't like to be given the same food day in, day out."

If a dog is resting or injured, and Charlie knows it will not be racing in the immediate future, he will provide a change of diet.

"I sometimes cut out the meat for one day and feed tripe instead. It rests the digestive system, and it gives the dogs a bit of variety, which I think they appreciate."

MENUS

Breakfast
(8.30am)

- Cereal (a mixture of cornflakes and Weetabix)
- 1 egg
- Spoonful of honey
- Milk (powdered)
- Served warm

Pre-Race Meal
(2-2.30pm)

- Cereal
- Spoonful of honey
- Glucose
- Milk
- Raw meat (to taste)

Main Meal
(2-2.30pm)

- Red Mills or Wafcol (changed to provide variety)
- Dogs: 1lb meat, cooked for resters or less active dogs. A proportion of the meat is fed raw for dogs competing
- Bitches: 12oz meat
- Brown bread
- Vegetable stew (meat stock, carrots, cabbage, pasta)
- Vitamin C tablet
- SA37 or multi-vitamin supplement
- Total weight of feed: 2 lbs

Post-Race Meal

- Water with electrolytes
- En route home: Milk
- Back in kennels: Main meal

CHAPTER EIGHT

GROOMING AND MASSAGE

As a breed, the greyhound has a low-maintenance coat. It is fine and close, and apart from dealing with the coat shedding, little more than routine grooming is required.

However, grooming is very much a dual-purpose operation. It keeps the coat in good order, and also offers the handler the opportunity to give the dog a routine check-up. If signs of trouble are spotted at an early stage, treatment can begin before the problem gets worse. This is important for any dog, but if you are dealing with a canine athlete, it is an essential part of the regular care regime.

GROOMING ROUTINE

At Mudros, all the greyhounds are groomed every day. Charlie teaches his staff a routine, and this is carried out meticulously. Charlie reckons that at least 15 minutes should be allocated to each dog for basic grooming.

"If we are very busy, the resters and retired dogs will have slightly less time spent on them, or we may occasionally miss a day with them. But if that happens, we make sure the dog is given a full grooming the following day."

COAT CARE

Each greyhound is given a thorough grooming with a bristle brush. If the dog is dirty, a hard bristle brush will remove dried mud. A soft bristle brush will be adequate for general grooming.

Every trainer develops his own routine, but the most important point is to groom

COAT CARE

Firstly, a bristle brush is used to give the greyhound a thorough grooming. This also gives an opportunity to check overall condition.

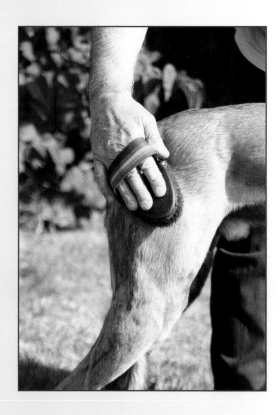

A hound glove will loosen dead hair, and will bring out the shine in the coat.

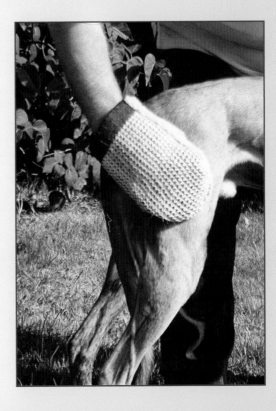

every part of the dog. For this reason, it is logical to start at the front and work your way down the body to the hindquarters.

"When you are grooming, you can check the condition of the skin, and the overall condition of the coat. A dog's coat is a very good indicator of health, so it is worth noting. You can also check for any unusual lumps or bumps – or anything that looks out of the ordinary. If you know what is normal for each greyhound, you will be quick to spot if anything is wrong."

Charlie then goes over the coat using a hound glove. This brings out the shine in the coat and loosens dead hair when the coat is shedding.

"We massage our racing dogs, but going over the coat with a hound glove does have a massaging effect, and helps the circulation."

BATHING

In the summer, the dogs are bathed every three weeks or so. A cast-iron bath, discarded from Charlie's house, makes an ideal dog bath. After bathing, the dogs are given a good rub down with a towel, and are then dried off with a hair dryer.

"I like the dogs to be bathed regularly – it freshens them up. It is particularly important for dogs that live in kennels."

Much of Charlie's training strategy is based on his belief that a dog must feel well in himself in order to perform to the best of his ability. For this reason, he will bath a dog two or three days before a big final.

In the winter, bathing is kept to a minimum. Instead, a dog will be sponged down with warm water. This freshens up the coat, but the dog does not risk getting cold from a complete soaking.

EYES

The eyes should be examined as part of the general check. They should be bright and sparkling, with no sign of discharge. Gently pull down the lower eyelid and check that there is no redness or inflammation.

NOSE

The nose should be clean, with no crustiness of the nostrils, and no discharge. A wet nose is not necessarily a sign of good health – it simply means that the dog licks his nose a lot!

EARS

The ears should be checked to ensure they are clean and smell fresh. Charlie's staff check ears on a daily basis and clean them

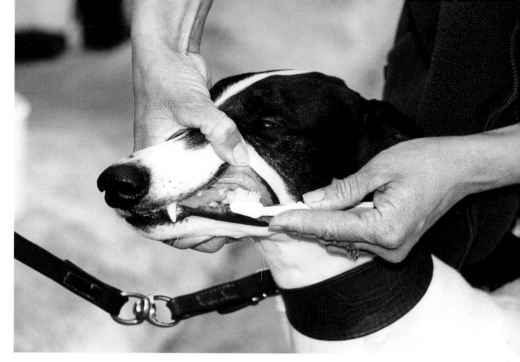

Teeth are brushed to prevent the accumulation of tartar.

when necessary, using cotton wool buds, soaked in a solution of water and TCP. Excessive dirt, or foul odour, could indicate an ear infection (see page 158).

DENTAL CARE

The diet that is fed at Mudros is generally soft, and so daily teeth-cleaning is essential to prevent the accumulation of tartar and the incidence of gum disease.

"We use a mixture of water, peroxide and toothpaste, and apply it with a long-handled toothbrush. The dogs get used to having their teeth cleaned, and they don't seem to mind at all," said Charlie.

He believes that giving a marrow bone is an excellent way of keeping teeth in good order, as well as giving the dog something to do.

"We clean the teeth every day, but sometimes you find that there is a build-up of tartar, which is difficult to remove. In that case, I would let that dog have a marrow bone."

If dogs are kennelled together, one of the dogs is removed while the other has a bone.

FOOT CARE

Foot care is vitally important for the racing greyhound. Both nails and pads must be checked on a daily basis in the kennels, and they must also be attended to after racing.

"When a dog comes off the track, we wash the feet in water and use a brush to remove sand from around the nails. It is the salt in the sand in the winter that causes problems with sore quicks (see page 172). It varies with the type of sand that is

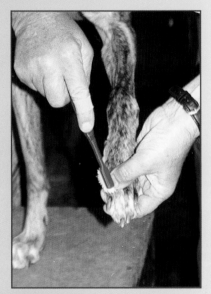

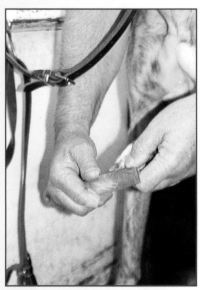

A brush is used to clean between the toes and the pads.

Nails need to be trimmed on a regular basis.

A file can be used, which avoids the risk of cutting into the quick.

used – the coarser it is, the more it can cause abrasions on the pads." (See page 171)

In the kennels, feet are checked and cleaned as part of the grooming regime. Charlie uses a small brush to clean between the toes and the pads, and this also gives the opportunity to check for any cracks or cuts on the pads (see page 170).

The nails must be kept short. Long nails can easily cause injury. Even if a greyhound is regularly exercised on hard surfaces, he will still need to have his nails trimmed on a regular basis.

There are two ways to trim nails: you can use guillotine nail-clippers, or a nail file. It is important not to cut into the quick of the nail. This is easy to see in white nails, but it is impossible to see on dark-coloured nails. If you cut into the quick, it will bleed copiously. This is obviously uncomfortable for the greyhound, and the dog may dislike having his nails trimmed in future.

"I teach the kennel staff to use a nail file. It may look big and cumbersome, but it is far better, as you cannot cut into the quick. You can file off the tip of the nail, and, in time, you learn how far you need to trim back. Then, when you are confident, you can use nail-clippers."

MASSAGE

The art of massage is an important part of preparing a dog for racing. Trainers may vary in their methods, but most share a common belief in the benefits of this form of therapy.

"It was Joe Booth who first showed me how to massage a greyhound," said Charlie. "I used to watch him working over a dog, and I picked it up from him."

The tools of the trade are very simple: embrocation oil and a skilful pair of hands. Using a firm, but sensitive technique, Charlie uses the ends of his fingers to massage deep into the muscles.

"I think it helps if you picture the muscles while you are massaging," he said.

The major benefit is to improve the blood supply to the muscles. It is also useful for detecting any soreness. Charlie has a wooden block in his grooming area, and his greyhounds are taught to stand with their front legs on the block. This enables Charlie to work on the underside of the dog without undue effort.

"The dogs love being massaged. I think they would stand there all day if you let them."

Charlie reckons it takes around 20 minutes to give a dog a full massage. He believes the work on a dog should take place at home, and not at the track.

"If a dog is prone to cramp, I might give the back muscles a quick rub down before a race, but there is no point in going over the top. You see some trainers putting all their energy into massaging the dog before he goes into the traps, and I always think: 'You've left that a bit late'."

Generally, greyhounds are given a thorough massage the day before a big race, and again on the morning of a final.

POST-RACE CHECK-UP

If a dog has run in a race, the following morning he is given a thorough check.

"If the dog has an obvious injury after a race, we would attend to him straight away. But we make a point of checking over each dog the following morning regardless of whether they have come off the track sound."

Charlie will run his hands over the dog's body, and flex and extend the joints to check if the dog is experiencing pain. Special attention is paid to the feet and nails to ensure that no injury has been sustained when racing.

Sand can be a real irritant, and so it is essential to wash the feet thoroughly.

STEP-BY-STEP GUIDE TO MASSAGE

Charlie has designed a wooden platform, so that a greyhound can stand comfortably while he is being massaged, and Charlie can reach every part of the dog.

Charlie starts by spraying embrocation oil on his hands.

He rubs the oil into his palms.

Sensitive use of the fingers is essential.

Starting at the front, Charlie works down the body.

The underside receives attention.

Working down over the loins.

It is important to keep the palms well lubricated.

Massaging the stifle and thigh.

Moving down the hind leg.

The inside and outside of each leg is massaged.

The treatment continues right down to the foot.

POST-RACE CHECK-UP

The morning after racing, every greyhound is checked for soreness or injury. This involves flexing and extending the joints, and feeling over the body for any sensitive areas.

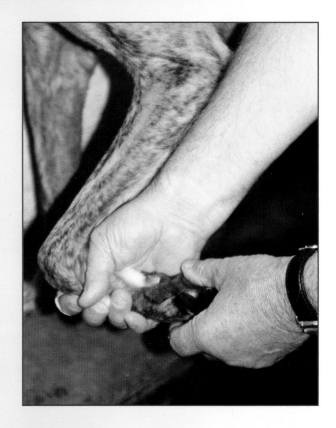

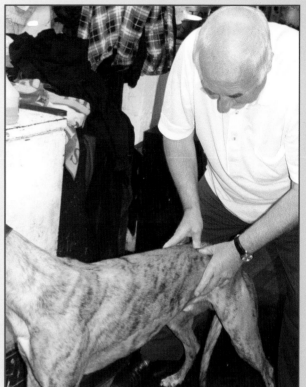

CHAPTER NINE

EXERCISE

If a greyhound is to perform to his full potential, he must be at peak fitness. The skill of the trainer is in discovering what exercise an individual dog needs in order to be in prime condition.

The racing greyhound must be well muscled so that he can corner or stretch out with ground-covering strides, as required. Equally important, the greyhound's cardio-vascular capacity must be built up so that the heart and lungs can operate effectively under the stress of racing.

That represents a big challenge, but the trainer of a racing greyhound has a further consideration. If a dog is competing in several rounds of a big competition, he must keep something in reserve, so that he leaves his best race for the final.

ROAD WALKING

Road walking is viewed as an important part of the exercise regime at the Mudros kennels.

"We use the lanes that run through woods, alongside the kennels," said Charlie. "There's always plenty to see, with squirrels and pheasants, and it keeps the dogs alert. If a dog is kept in kennels, it is very important to give him some mental stimulation. If you watch a dog out on a walk, you will see his ears pricked, and he is looking around. He is stepping out and using his muscles, but he is also using his brain.

"Generally, the dogs are walked for a mile or a mile and a half. It depends on how much time we have. But a good 30 minutes' walk will work well for most greyhounds."

Walking gives the dogs a change of scene, as well as building up fitness.

Charlie has a trap, but he generally handslips greyhounds on the gallop. Here, assistant, trainer Chris Akers has just released a dog.

There is a rule that no more than two dogs are walked at a time.

"I know some trainers will exercise four dogs at a time. But I think it is too risky. You only need something unexpected to happen – like a pheasant starting up in front of you – and you can lose control."

Variety is the spice of life. Charlie will road walk a greyhound two or three times a week, and on the other days the dog will be given a gallop.

"It all depends on what the dog is doing, and what he needs at a particular time. If a dog is returning from injury, we would start by giving a few road walks to begin with before stepping up to faster work. I also like to use road walking when a dog is building up to a big final, as it can sharpen him up."

GALLOPING

Charlie has a 250-yard (230m) gallop, and it is probably the most valuable stretch of land at Mudros. It gives him an opportunity to watch how a greyhound runs, as well as to work on fitness. It has also been used to help a greyhound to overcome trapping problems (see page 144).

Charlie has worked on the surface so that the gallop is now as near-perfect a running surface as possible. He brought in a large quantity of Irish peat and rotivated it into the ground before levelling it. The grass surface is kept relatively short.

"The peat has helped the drainage enormously. It helps to retain moisture so the surface does not become too hard. Even when we have a hot, dry spell, it is generally okay without additional watering."

Charlie has a fine eye for judging dogs on the gallop – and he makes many important decisions based on what he sees at home.

Charlie does not use a drag hare, as he believes that it encourages a dog to pull up too fast.

"A dog risks jarring himself if he stops too quickly, so I prefer to use a squeaker. I stand at the top of the gallop, and one of the lads will either handslip a dog or release him from a trap. That gives me a really good opportunity of watching the dog run."

The amount of galloping given to a greyhound depends on his racing programme.

"I would keep a greyhound at racing fitness by galloping him twice a week. But in some competitions, where it is tight between rounds, I wouldn't gallop the dog so often. It all depends on the individual – some need more work than others in order to get fit, or to maintain fitness (see Chapter 9).

"If a dog is returning from injury, we build up fitness gradually. Rather than trying the dog over the full 250-yard gallop, we would try him over a shorter distance – say half-way up – until we were confident that the dog was sound and could cope with the full gallop.

"I find that the gallop is a great time-saver, as, in many cases, we can use it to see how a greyhound is running rather than having to travel to a track for a trial."

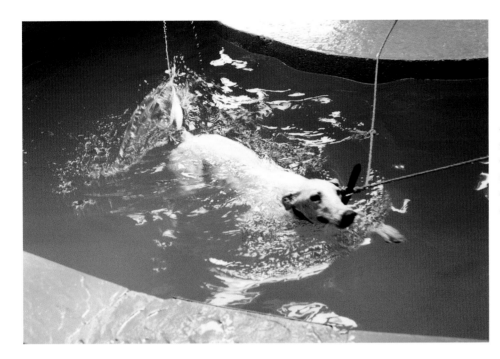

Swimming is a great form of exercise for greyhounds returning from injury.

SWIMMING

Swimming has proved to be an excellent form of exercise for greyhounds returning from injury. Charlie has a facility he uses locally that specialises in this type of therapy for injured dogs.

The dogs are walked down a ramp into the pool. The sides of the pool are equipped with water jets, and so the dog has to swim against the flow of the water.

"A minute's swimming is as much as most dogs need. It is very hard work, swimming against the water. We usually take a few dogs at a time, and they really benefit from it. It is a way of exercising without any strain."

After the swimming session, the dogs are dried off with large purpose-built dryers.

"Most of the dogs I have taken there love it. They are sometimes a bit apprehensive to begin with, but they really like it when they get used to the idea."

CHAPTER TEN

THE OPEN RACE CIRCUIT

The majority of greyhound trainers operate between two bases – the kennels and their home track, with the occasional raid on an open race competition. Charlie Lister is one of only a handful of trainers not contracted to a track, and so he does not have to be concerned with providing dogs to fill racecards. He has the freedom to run his dogs wherever he chooses, whenever he wants.

However, Charlie, and his owners, are in the business of winning races, and so rather than getting to know one track, and producing dogs to suit it, Charlie needs to exploit every big race opportunity that comes his way. That means having a detailed knowledge of all the tracks in the UK, so that he knows which dogs will be best suited to a particular circuit.

"To a certain extent, we are influenced by geography. We would not go to the most far-flung tracks unless there was a good reason for it," said Charlie. "But, having said that, an open race trainer must be prepared to travel."

Charlie clocks up a phenomenal number of miles each year. The van he has had for two years has done more than 110,000 miles. His other van has a mileage of 50,000 in just over a year. Then there are the miles he drives in his own car, which he takes when he only has a couple of greyhounds racing.

"Sometimes an owner will want a dog to run at a particular track, or take part in a certain competition because they want to see the dog run. But, mostly, the owners let me decide what is best for the dog.

Travelling is a way of life if you have a small, select string of racing greyhounds.

PLANNING A CAMPAIGN

Charlie likes to have a master plan for each of his racing dogs. Although this may have to be changed, depending on fitness and injury, he always works out a long-term strategy.

"When it comes to late December/early January when there is frost on the ground, I start planning for the coming year. I don't like to race too many good dogs in those conditions, so it gives the dogs a break, and I have a chance to think.

"When I am considering whether to enter a greyhound for a competition, I think about the dog's style of running. You may have a fast dog in the kennel, but you have to work out if that dog can perform to the best of his ability at a particular track. The only exception is the Derby –

every owner of a top-class dog wants his dog to compete in the Derby.

"But generally, I will look at how a dog runs, and I will have a good idea of what will suit him. You need to consider not only the distance, but how a dog copes with sharp bends, whether he has early pace, whether he is a strong running type that suits a big galloping track, or whether you have a sprinter that might come good on a tighter circuit.

"There are some tracks that definitely favour railers. The big, galloping tracks, with wide bends, are not always the best bet for wide runners. A wide runner will tend to run as wide as possible, and a tighter track will help to hold the dog in.

"I am lucky enough to have won big races at most of the tracks. To a large

In the dark winter months of December and January, Charlie plans his open race campaign.

extent, it is a matter of picking the right dog for the right track. For example, Belle Vue has a long run to the first bend, but the first bend is pretty sharp. To be able to run that, you need a railer."

It is also important to assess a greyhound's ability to stay. It may be that a dog starts his career over four bends, and then graduates to six.

"Mostly you can tell quite easily if a dog is going to stay, but there are times when you can be fooled. Droopys Slave won the Puppy Cup at Belle Vue over 460m, and then won the All England Cup at Brough Cup over 480m in consecutive years. He was running on very strong over 500m, so I thought he would stay 630m. But when we tried him, he didn't get the distance."

The type of hare is also a consideration. The majority of tracks now have a Swaffham hare, but this type of lure has had its fair share of critics.

"There are those that think the Swaffham hare is not noisy enough, and this can cause dogs to fight. Personally, I don't think it is a problem if a dog is genuine, but it can be hard on the youngsters who are just learning what to expect."

TRACK SURFACES

Every track has its own idiosyncrasies in terms of the shape of the circuit, the distance to the first bend, and the camber of the track. It is down to the skill of the trainer to decide whether a greyhound can perform to his full potential at a particular venue. However, there is a further consideration, which can affect how a dog runs – the surface.

"I liked the all-grass tracks. There was no better sight than White City on Derby final night when it was an all-grass surface. But now we have so much more racing, it doesn't make sense. You have to have an all-weather surface.

"There was a time when a few tracks went in for grass straights and sanded

Charlie reckons there were fewer injuries when greyhounds ran on grass tracks.

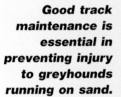

Good track maintenance is essential in preventing injury to greyhounds running on sand.

bends. That worked okay for track dogs who were used to the circuit. But when I went open racing with dogs that were not familiar with the circuit, they were at a disadvantage. I found that some dogs would break their stride as they came off the sand bend.

"We didn't get as many injuries on grass tracks. We used to get a few toe injuries, but on sand we get more muscle injuries. Sore muscles and pulled muscles are pretty common, and I think we get more broken hocks than we used to."

Charlie is a firm believer that good track maintenance can make a huge difference to the incidence of injury.

"Different types of sand are used, and that can affect the going. Sand needs plenty of water to give it a good, even surface, but some types of sand do not hold the water, and it tends to move on the surface.

"Hove has a brilliant running surface, and that all comes down to using the right type of sand, and ensuring that the drainage is effective."

There was a memorable occasion in 2001 when Charlie faced a stewards' inquiry for withdrawing Romany Joe from a 620m open race at Milton Keynes.

"We had a terrible time. A dog called Shanahan broke his hock in a trial, and then Go Ahead Joe did a tendon behind his wrist in a 440m open. Both injuries happened at virtually the same place. After Shanahan was injured I went to look at the track, and I wasn't very happy with what I saw. The sand was very loose on top, and the dogs were going in quite a way. I told the groundsman, but nothing was done. I decided I didn't want to risk running my dogs."

Milton Keynes subsequently carried out improvements to the track, and, as far as Charlie is concerned, it is all water under the bridge. But it does illustrate the fact that Charlie always puts the welfare of his greyhounds first.

"I like Milton Keynes, and the track is fine now. But when something like that happens, you have to be prepared to stand up for what you think is right."

ALL-TIME FAVOURITES

Open race trainers have their favourite tracks, and Charlie is no exception.

"Yarmouth has always been a lucky track for me. My wife, Val, and I used to go for a holiday down there during the festival, and we would take a couple of dogs to try to recoup our expenses.

"It started when I was flapping, and we

Another East Anglian Derby victory at Charlie's favourite track – Yarmouth. On this occasion it's Terrydrum Kate who takes honours.

would try to bring a dog with top acceleration – usually a sprinter. We found that if a dog could get out and miss the trouble behind, he had a good chance, even if he didn't quite stay the trip."

Charlie has now won the East Anglian Derby a record seven times.

"I love going down there. We are always made to feel welcome, and we meet up with lots of old friends. They keep the surface really well, and we have had a lot of success. It is an ideal track for a good railing dog."

In terms of distance, Nottingham is Charlie's local track, and as well as competing in major competitions, he uses it for trialling youngsters, and for dogs returning to the track after injury or after a rest.

"Nottingham is an excellent track. I honestly believe that if it had the facilities, it would be rated as one of the top tracks in the country. The surface is kept in very good condition, and I have no fault to find with it. Over the years, I have put every one of my best dogs round Nottingham. If you get beat there, you are beaten by a better dog."

Monmore Green also rates very highly in Charlie's book: "It is the type of track where you can see a dog perform at his best. It's an easy running circuit, and the surface is maintained very well."

Like many trainers, Charlie mourns the demise of White City, but when staging a big event, no track compares with Wimbledon.

"It is the only track that can cope with the huge Derby crowd, and the facilities are pretty good. I'm much happier with the track since improvements were carried out.

"At the first bend, the inside rail stuck out a shade, and, to my mind, it was causing problems. The inside dog had to come out to steer clear of the rail, and this often meant interfering with another dog. This was also the case at the 480m traps. The one dog had to come out, and this caused the two dog to check. I spoke to Bob Rowe (Wimbledon's Racing Manager) about it, and, after looking at the rail, they made changes. I think the track runs a lot better now."

TRACK KENNELS
When racegoers attend a meeting, they see the 'public face' of the track. Generally, everything looks spick and span, and most racegoers are more interested in the catering facilities than bothering about what goes on behind the scenes.

But for trainers with dogs to care for, it is the facilities that are not open to the public that are the most important. The standard of track kennels and exercise areas varies enormously, and Charlie is infuriated by sub-standard conditions.

Charlie puts the welfare of his greyhounds beyond all other considerations.

"There are some tracks where the kennels are in a diabolical state. When you think of the money they spend on carpeting the bar, or extending the restaurant, it doesn't make sense. They should be looking after the dogs – after all, they are providing the entertainment."

At some tracks, such as Walthamstow and Nottingham, the kennels are heated, and there is a cooling system that can be used in hot weather. But, at most of the tracks, there are no such facilities. The biggest problem is an unheated kennel in winter, where a greyhound may have to be confined for several hours. "All you can do is put the dog in a good kennel coat, but it is far from ideal," he said.

He is also critical of the paddocks at most tracks. "They are often small and dirty, and you don't really want to take a greyhound in there. When you think that something like a hundred dogs are using that paddock on a race night, it is ridiculous. It would not cost much to provide something decent."

KENNELLING TIMES

In the UK, dogs are usually kennelled at around 5.30pm, prior to the evening's racing.

"If you have dogs that are racing early on in the evening, that is fair enough. But if a dog is not racing until 10pm, he has four hours in the kennel. That is far too long. In Ireland, they allow a later kennelling time – usually about 7pm – which makes far more sense.

"The worst thing is if you are stuck in traffic, which can happen at any time. You ring up the track and explain the situation, but all they say is: 'If you miss kennelling, the dog cannot race'. You could have travelled halfway across the country, and it would still make no difference.

"There was some sense to early kennelling when all dogs were tested before racing, but now, with testing on a random basis, it makes no sense at all."

Charlie has had a few nightmare journeys, battling with traffic, to get to a track on time. But none was worse than the time he was stranded in Holyhead with two dogs – one of them Rapid Ranger – before the start of the 2000 Irish Derby.

"It was the first round of the Irish Derby, and there was a huge amount of money on Rapid Ranger as he was up for the treble. He had already won the Scottish and English Derbies, and he was on a bonus to get all three.

"We had planned to travel during the day, and Rapid Ranger was racing that evening. But the weather got worse and worse, and the ferry before ours was cancelled. That meant we couldn't get a place on the ferry we had booked.

"I was in a real panic, because I knew how much money was on Rapid Ranger. I rang up Ray White, the owner, and he said he could arrange for a helicopter to take us over. Then I really started to panic. I had never been in a helicopter before, and I didn't really fancy it. I also thought it would upset the dogs.

"I got in touch with Shelbourne Park, and they spoke to the ferry people. They told them that there were thousands of pounds resting on the dog getting to Ireland, and we had to be given a place. They let us on, and we were met off the ferry with a police escort, which accompanied us to Shelbourne Park.

"We got there just in time, and we managed to qualify the dog. But I was absolutely shattered – my nerves were completely on edge."

CHARLIE'S GUIDE TO BRITAIN'S TRACKS

BELLE VUE

- **Track circumference:** 395m
- **Hare:** Outside Swaffham
- **Distances raced:** 237m, 465m, 465mh, 647m, 875m
- **Run to first bend:** 103m (465m)
- **Charlie's record:** Manchester Puppy Cup

1979 (Meanus Duke); 1983 (Spots Of Condor); 1992 (Droopys Slave); Cesarewitch 1993 (Killeenagh Dream); Cock O' The North 1993 (Monard Wish); Gorton Cup 1994 (Just Right Kyle); Northern Oaks 1995 (Egmont Joan); Rapid Raceline Invitation 1995 (Stouke Whisper); Northern Flat 1997 (Brannigan's Gig);

Stayers Grand 1998 (Drumsna Power); Northern Oaks 1998 (Terrydrum Kate), 2003 (Bower Agnes); Laurels 1999 (Derbay Flyer); Dransfield Stayers 2002 (Knockaun Joker).
- **Track records still standing:** 2001 Parliament Act (16.63 metres per second).

❝ *I have won most of the big races at Belle Vue, and I like going there. There is a long run to the first bend, so you need a dog with early pace. I would always prefer to run a railer here. Belle Vue is a good galloping track with sharp corners. Personally, I would always like to give a dog a trial before racing.* ❞

BROUGH PARK

- **Track circumference:** 415m
- **Hare:** Outside Sumner
- **Distances raced:** 480m, 500m, 640m
- **Run to first bend:** 130m (480m)
- **Charlie's record:** Northumberland Gold Cup 1993 and 1994 (Droopys Slave); Heineken Puppy Trophy 1994 (Chadwell Charmer); All England Cup 1997 (Endon Tiger), 1999 (Derbay Flyer); 2000 (Tobermorey Boy).

❝ *A good galloping track, which is better suited to railers. The first bend is very tight, and the dogs on the outside tend to bunch up and find trouble.* ❞

COVENTRY

- **Track circumference:** 400m

- **Hare:** Sealey Hare
- **Distances raced:** 280m, 480m, 680m, 880m
- **Run to first bend:** 93m (480m)

❝ *I don't offer praise easily, it has to be deserved, but the people at Coventry have tried really hard, and the place deserves to be a success. It's a brilliant running track, very safe, and a good gallop.* ❞

CRAYFORD

- **Track circumference:** 334m
- **Hare:** Swaffham
- **Distances raced:** 380m, 540m, 714m, 874m, 1048m
- **Run to first bend:** 77m (380m; 77m (540m)
- **Charlie's record:** First Radio Luxembourg Invitation Stakes 1982 (Yellow Cowboy).

❝ *I have to admit, I have only been to Crayford once. Obviously, it's quite a distance to travel, but it's not my type of track. The circuit is very tight with sharp bends. It's the sort of track where a top-class dog can get beaten by a grader. There is always likely to be trouble.* ❞

HALL GREEN

- **Track circumference:** 412m
- **Hare:** Swaffham McGee
- **Distances raced:** 258m, 480m, 645m, 670m, 820m, 892m
- **Run to first bend:** 85m (480m)
- **Charlie's record:** Archie Scott Memorial

Trophy 1993 (Just Right Kyle); Midland Flat Championship 1993 (Just Right Kyle);1999 (Westmead Striker), 2000 (Wise Emerald); Midland Oaks 1993 (Simply Free),1999 (Alannas Spark), 2001 (Call Me Baby); Blue Riband 2003 (Farloe Verdict); Gymcrack Puppy Championship 2003 (Moynies Cash).

- **Track records still standing:** 2003 Farloe Verdict 480m 28.09 (17.09 metres per second).

6 *I like Hall Green – it's a much better track since they did work on the bends and installed the Swaffham hare. They keep the track very well. I always used to trial a dog there before a competition, but now I don't think it is necessary. I would always favour a good early-paced railer here.* 9

HARLOW

- **Track circumference:** 354m
- **Hare:** Outside Swaffham
- **Distances raced:** 238m, 415m, 592m, 769m, 946m

6 *I have been to the track a couple of times for a look round, and it seems to be kept in good condition.* 9

HENLOW

- **Track circumference:** 410m
- **Hare:** Outside Swaffham
- **Distances raced:** 250m, 460m, 550m, 660m, 870m, 960m

- **Run to first bend:**75m
- **Charlie's record:** Bedfordshire Derby 1985 (Glamour Hobo).

6 *It's a funny shape, but the track has a good surface. It is a short run to the first corner, and then it's like a straight between the third and the fourth bends. I haven't been there often, but I like going there.* 9

HOVE

- **Track circumference:** 455m
- **Hare:** Swaffham
- **Distances raced:** 285m, 475m, 515m, 695m, 740m, 930m, 970m
- **Run to first bend:** 105m (4 bends)
- **Charlie's record:** The Regency 1995 (Suncrest Sail); Teamtalk.com Trophy 2001 (Sexy Delight); Tomsthebest.com 2002 (True Honcho); MDC Alvin PR Applause Stakes 2003 (Farloe Bonus).

6 *This is a very good track. I liked it when it was a grass track, but it runs just as well with sand. They keep the surface in top-class condition. It is the type of track where you can take a dog without trialling him first. A dog can come from behind, as long as it has a bit of pace and stays.* •9

HULL

Track circumference: 415m
- **Hare:** Fannon Swaffham
- **Distances raced:** 240m, 460m, 490m, 655m, 875m

* **Run to first bend:** 90m (490m)
* **Charlie's record:** Dean Jackson Memorial Trophy 1995 (Harrys Boy Blue).

6 *Even though it's not very far to travel, I haven't gone to Hull a great deal. I wasn't that keen on the surface, and I didn't like the run to the first bend. I'm looking forward to taking a look at the new track.* 9

KINSLEY

* **Track circumference:** 380m
* **Hare:** Outside Swaffham
* **Distances raced:** 275m, 450m, 485m, 656m, 866m

6 *I used to go to Kinsley in the old days when it was a flapping track, but since it has switched to NGRC, there are not the competitions to go for. They have made quite a few alterations, and I believe the track runs much better – I remember it used to run downhill into the bend.* 9

MILDENHALL

* **Track circumference:** 325m
* **Hare:** Outside Sumner
* **Distances raced:** 220m, 375m, 545m, 730m, 870m, 1025m
* **Run to first bend:** 70m (375m)

6 *It's not very handy for me, but I have been there a few times. It's a small, round track with no straights. It doesn't suit fast dogs. You need the small, sprinting type.* 9

MILTON KEYNES

* **Track circumference:** 375m
* **Hare:** Swaffham McGee
* **Distances raced:** 245m, 440m, 620m, 815m
* **Run to first bend:** 60m (440m), 72m (620m)
* **Charlie's record:** Christmas Cracker 1998 (Gaytime Dean); Milton Keynes Summer Cup 1998, 1999 and 2000 (Farloe Bonus); Milton Keynes Derby 2002 (El Ronan).
* **Track records still standing:** 1998 Farloe Bonus 620m 37.86 (16.38 metres per second).

6 *I have been going to Milton Keynes for years. I've won the Derby there, and I won the Summer Cup three times with Farloe Bonus. It's a handy little track, but you need to give a dog a trial there first. I like to take youngsters there to give them a bit of experience. You need an early paced dog who will run off the bends and accelerate down the straights.* 9

MONMORE GREEN

* **Track circumference:** 419m
* **Hare:** Swaffham
* **Distances raced:** 364m, 480m, 630m, 835m, 900m
* **Charlie's record:** Midland St. Leger 1995 (Dinan Wonder); Ellen Killen Standard 1997 (Dragon Knight); Ladbroke Sporting Sprint 1997 (Cry Havoc); Caffreys New Track Trophy (King Oscar); Christmas

Puppy Cracker 2001 (Droopys Prowler); Ladbroke Festival 2002 (Seskin Rocket); Ladbroke Gold Cup 2003 (Farloe Brazil).
* **Track records still standing:** 1997 Cry Havoc 210m 12.64 (16.61 metres per second); 2001 Parliament Act 264m 15.32 (17.23 metres per second).

❝ This is a lovely track with good, long straights and easy running bends. The surface is kept very well. I have won quite a few competitions there – the Gold Cup with Farloe Brazil sticks in my mind. You want a nice, pacey dog to run here, but a dog can come through and win from behind. ❞

NOTTINGHAM

* **Track circumference:** 437m
* **Hare:** Outside Swaffham McGee
* **Distances raced:** 300m, 480m, 500m, 722m, 730m, 902m
* **Run to first bend:** 85m (500m), 55m (730m)
* **Charlie's record:** Coldseal Puppy Classic 1994 (Callahow Daly), 1999 (Kit Kat Kid); Peter Derrick National Sprint Championship 1996 (Some Picture), 1999 (Gulleen Slaney); Know Something Stakes 1997 (Some Picture); Ladbrokes Freephone Sprint Trophy 2002 (Soviet King); Ladbroke Dotcom Puppy Trophy 2002 (Toms Autumn); John Smith's Breeders Puppy Cup 2003 (Farloe Brazil); Fosters National Oaks 2003 (Knocktoosh Queen); Bookmakers Guineas 2003 (Top Savings).
* **Track records still standing:** 2004 Bell

Legend 500m 29.69

❝ This is my local track, and I have had a lot of success here over the years. It's also the track where I trial a lot of my dogs. There is a good run to the first corner, and a nice back straight. You want a strong running dog, but a dog does not have to lead to win – it can come from behind. ❞

OXFORD

* **Track circumference:** 395m
* **Hare:** Swaffham
* **Distances raced:** 250m, 450m, 595m, 645m, 845m, 1040m
* **Run to first bend:** 100m (4 bends), 90m (6 bends)
* **Charlie's record:** William Hill Gold Cup 2001 (El Ronan).

❝ You definitely want a railer here. If you look at the record, the percentage of outside dogs winning is not great. It's a nice track, although the first bend is a bit sharp. All the same, it's a track I like going to. ❞

PERRY BARR

* **Track circumference:** 434m
* **Hare:** Outside Sumner
* **Distances raced:** 275m, 480m, 660m, 710m, 895m
* **Run to first bend:** 80m (4 bends), 50m (6 bends)
* **Charlie's record:** Birmingham Cup 1999 (Derbay Flyer).

- **Track records still standing:** 2003 Burberry Boy 480m 28.45 (16.87 metres per second).

6 *This is a good running track. They have made quite a few improvements, and now they have a good surface. You need a strong running type who definitely gets 480m.* 9

PETERBOROUGH

- **Track circumference:** 370m
- **Hare:** Outside Swaffham
- **Distances raced:** 235m, 420m, 605m, 790m, 975m
- **Run to first bend:** 80m (4 bends)
- **Charlie's record:** Peterborough Cesarewitch 1990 (Slideaway Snoopy); Peterborough Puppy Derby 1993 (Sure Fantasy); Peterborough Puppy Cesarewitch 2001 (Farloe Totty).

6 *This is a track I have gone to for years. It's a circuit for a specialist dog. You need a dog that is very fast away, as it is a short run to the corner.* 9

POOLE

- **Track circumference:** 450m
- **Hare:** Outside Swaffham
- **Distances raced:** 250m, 450m, 640m, 840m

6 *Apologies to Poole – but I've never been there.* 9

PORTSMOUTH

- **Track circumference:** 354m
- **Hare:** Inside Sumner
- **Distances raced:** 438m, 610m, 792m, 964m
- **Run to first bend:** 90m (438m), 95m (610m)
- **Major open events:** Golden Muzzle.

6 *There's no real reason for it, but I've never made it to Portsmouth, either.* 9

READING

- **Track circumference:** 385m
- **Hare:** Outside Sumner
- **Distances raced:** 275m, 465m, 660m, 850m, 1045m
- **Run to first bend:** 80m (465m)

6 *I have been here a couple of times. The circuit is pretty tight and the bends are sharp.* 9

ROMFORD

- **Track circumference:** 350m
- **Hare:** Outside Swaffham
- **Distances raced:** 225m, 400m, 575m, 750m, 925m
- **Run to first bend:** 67m (400m and 575m)
- **Charlie's record:** Racing Post Puppy Cup 1997 (Ballyard Recruit); Quicksilver Stakes 1997 (King Oscar); Golden Sprint 1997 (King Oscar).

❝ It is a pretty tight track, and so you really need a fast-up railer. ❞

RYE HOUSE

Track circumference: 420m
Hare: Swaffham
Distances raced: 265m, 445m, 485m, 630m, 685m
Run to first bend: 80m (4 bends), 40m (6 bends)

❝ I went there years ago, and I had to pay for a kennel hand to get in – I haven't been back there since. ❞

SHAWFIELD

- **Track circumference:** 432m
- **Hare:** Swaffham
- **Distances raced:** 330m, 450m, 480m, 480mh, 500m, 670m, 730m, 882m, 932m
- **Run to first bend:** 100m (300m), 90m (500m)
- **Charlie's record:** William King Cup 1993 (Spenwood Magic), 1996 (Suncrest Sail); Daily Record Marathon 1994 (Sunhill Misty); Regal St. Leger 1995 (Suncrest Sail); Regal Stayers 1999 (Foxcover Lizzie); Scottish Derby 1997 (Some Picture) 2003 (Micks Mystic), 2004 (Farloe Verdict).
- **Track records still standing:** 2004 Farloe Verdict 480m 28.79 (16.76 metres per second).

❝ This is a big, galloping track, and you need a strong dog who can stay the distance. It can be quite testing, as there is an uphill run to the winning line. ❞

SHEFFIELD

- **Track circumference:** 425m
- **Hare:** Outside Swaffham
- **Distances raced:** 280m, 362m, 480m, 500m, 500mh, 660m
- **Run to first bend:** 62m (500m)
- **Charlie's record:** Northern Sprint 1980 (Superior Champ, 1986 (Night Runner); 1992 (Bank Tunnel), 1995 (Tailors Noel), 2000 (Parliament Act), 2002 (Larkhill Bullet); Diamond Jubilee 500 1992 (Risk It Miss); Steel City Cup 1998 (Lyons Turbo); Yorkshire Oaks 1993 (Simply Free); Dransfield St. Leger 1993 (Spenwood Magic); November Grand 1993 (Sure Fantasy); Xmas Cup 1993 (Sure Fantasy); Dransfield Novelty Ebor 1994 (Tammys Delight), 1995 and 1996 (Suncrest Sail); Spring Cup 1999 (Colwins Glory); William Hill Stayers Classic 1999 (Farloe Bonus); Hardys Juvenile Invitation 1999 (Kit Kat Kid); Dransfield Lotteries Puppy Cup 1999 (Rapid Ranger); Hardy Bookmaker Champion Stakes Juvenile 2000 (Toblemorey Boy); JPV Bookmakers Category Two Stakes 2003 (Knocktoosh Queen), Coors Brewers Puppy Silver Collar 2004 (Bell Legend).
- **Track records still standing:** 1995 Suncrest Sail 730m 43.64 (16.73 metres per second); 1996 Suncrest Sail 660m 39.40 (16.75 metres per second); 1997 Farloe Bubble 360m 20.82 (17.39 metres

per second); 2000 Parliament Act 280m 16.38 (17.09 metres per second).

6 *I have won quite a lot here. It's a good running track with short straights and big, round bends. You need a fast-up dog that gets the trip.* 9

SITTINGBOURNE

- **Track circumference:** 443m
- **Hare:** Outside Swaffham
- **Distances raced:** 265m, 473m, 473mh, 642m, 708m, 916m

6 *I've only been to Sittingbourne once, and that was for the Trainers Championship. It's a track where you need to trial first, and, for me, that means too much travelling.* 9

STAINFORTH

- **Track circumference:** 438m
- **Hare:** Fannon Swaffham
- **Distances raced:** 278m, 480m, 666m, 709m, 888m, 925m
- **Run to first bend:** 105m (278m)

6 *This is a very good galloping track and the surface is kept well. I don't go there much, but that is only because there are no big open events.* 9

SUNDERLAND

- **Track circumference:** 378m
- **Hare:** Outside McGee

- **Distances raced:** 261m, 450m, 640m, 828m
- **Run to first bend:** 93m (450m), 84m (640m)
- **Charlie's record:** Sunderland Oaks 1990 (Slideaway Snoopy); Milligans Bakery Challenge 1992 (Callahow Daly); Puppy Trophy 1994 (Chadwell Charmer); 2002 (Farloe Forty) Regal Gold Cup 2002 (El Ronan).

6 *This is a funny track and a dog needs a couple of trials to get the hang of it. The bends are so wide, you need a dog who has good pace into the bend so he can run on. It suits sprinting types that like the rails.* 9

SWINDON

- **Track circumference:** 452m
- **Hare:** Swaffham McGee
- **Distances raced:** 285m, 460m, 480m, 480mh, 509m, 685m, 737m
- **Run to first bend:** 100m (509m)
- **Charlie's record:** BAS Guineas 1998 (Rather Special); Stan James Anniversary 500 2003 (Clear Run).

6 *This is a very good galloping track. I would say you get as good a gallop here as anywhere in the country. You definitely need a strong-running dog.* 9

WALTHAMSTOW

- **Track circumference:** 405m
- **Hare:** Swaffham

- **Distances raced:** 415m, 435m, 475m, 640m, 840m, 880m, 1045m
- **Run to first bend:** 100m (475m), 68m (640m)
- **Charlie's record:** Walthamstow Bookmakers Invitation 1994 (Monard Wish); Pepsi Cola Marathon 1994 (Sunhill Misty); NGRC Stewards Cup 1995 (Suncrest Sail); Grand Prix 1995 (Suncrest Sail), 1996 (Spring Rose); BBC TV Trophy 1996 (Suncrest Sail); 1998 (Dans Sport); Racing Post Festival Stakes 1998 (Dans Sport); Racing Post Puppy Stakes 2001 (Droopys Prowler); Stow Marathon 2001 (Sexy Delight).
- **Track records still standing:** 1996 Spring Rose 640m 39.05 (16.39 metres per second).

❝ Dogs need to trial round here as the first bend is very sharp. The surface is kept pretty well. It is a good training ground for puppies. ❞

WIMBLEDON

- **Track circumference:** 408m
- **Hare:** Outside Swaffham
- **Distances raced:** 252m, 460m, 480m, 660m, 680m, 868m, 1068m
- **Run to first bend:** 85.66m (4 bends)
- **Charlie's record:** Key 1993 (Killeenagh Dream); TV Trophy 2000 (Sexy Delight);

Greyhound Derby 1997 (Some Picture); 2000 and 2001 (Rapid Ranger), 2003 (Farloe Verdict).

❝ The track runs a lot better since alterations were made to the running rail and to the first bend, but you still need to trial here first. I would always want an early paced railer to run here. ❞

YARMOUTH

- **Track circumference:** 382m
- **Hare:** Swaffham
- **Distances raced:** 277m, 462m, 659m, 843m
- **Run to first bend:** 85m (462m)
- **Charlie's record:** Pepsi Cola Sprint 1987 (Jers Pick), 2001 (Parliament Act); East Anglian Derby 1981 (Swift Band), 1990 (Artie Joe), 1993 (Just Right Kyle), 1995 (Dragon Prince), 1997 (Terrydrum Kate), 2002 (Larkhill Bullet), 2003 (Burberry Boy); Wafcol East Anglian Challenge 1995 (Dragon Prince), 2001 (El Ronan); Derby Purse 2002 (Knockaun Joker).

❝ This has been a very lucky track for me, and I always love going to Yarmouth. I have now won seven East Anglian Derbies. There's a long run to the first corner, and then a nice, long back straight. Ideally, I would trial a dog here first. ❞

CHAPTER ELEVEN

THE BIG TIME

It takes a lot of expertise to plan a racing campaign for a top-class greyhound. It is not enough to pick the right competition, you also need to get the dog to the top of his form to give him every chance of winning.

"Open racing is much harder work than graded racing," said Charlie. "It's not just the travelling – it is the preparation of the dogs. You have to keep everything ticking over in your mind so that you are bringing a dog to peak fitness at the right time, and at the right pace."

RACE FITNESS

Charlie tends to rest his dogs in the worst of the winter, as he doesn't like them running in freezing conditions.

"I don't like to risk injury at that time of the year. The dogs need a break from racing, so it makes sense to rest them. You cannot expect a top dog to keep going all year round. When the dog is resting, I would change the diet, cutting out raw meat entirely. The aim is to keep the dog ticking over.

"I start to bring the dogs back in March with the Derby in mind. It is the biggest race in the calendar, and if you have a top-quality four-bend dog, you have to set your sights there. It is what every owner wants, even if they know, realistically, that their dog is unlikely to get very far. However, it is very hard to make your plans in March, and to get a dog spot-on for the Derby in June. You can put in all the work, and then the dog can go lame on you just before the competition starts.

RACE FITNESS

Charlie likes a greyhound to have scope for improvement at the start of a big competition.

A greyhound needs to be bought back to racing fitness gradually, starting with a gallop at home.

"I start introducing raw meat to the diet as the dogs come back into work. I would start with getting a dog fit at home with road walking and short gallops. I would then move on to sprint trials, and progress to a four-bend race. The aim is to bring the dog to a good level of fitness so that he is feeling well and confident.

"If a dog is entering a big competition, I would give him a trial first. But if that dog had already run at that track, I probably wouldn't bother. I might give a Derby contender a couple of trials at Wimbledon – it depends if the dog knows the track well or not. I do not use trials as a way of getting a dog fit. I do that by galloping the dog at home.

"Ideally, I like to see my dogs running at around 75 per cent of their best at the start of the Derby. You want the dog running well, but you must have plenty in reserve. You need to have some scope for improvement, and as the competition progresses, you can run the dog into full fitness.

"I give stayers more work in order to build up their stamina. I would make sure they had more walking exercise. A four-bend dog would need one or two gallops a week, depending on the dog, whereas a stayer would always need two gallops a week. You need to build up their stamina and their respiration."

ROUND BY ROUND

The work that is needed once a competition gets underway depends on how many runs there are in the contest, and the gap between each of the rounds.

"At the start of the Derby, I am not looking any further than qualifying. By the second round, the pace is beginning to hot up, and you need the dog to be running well."

When there is a reasonable gap between each of the rounds, Charlie will road walk his Derby contenders, and may give them a gallop.

"You want to keep the dog loose and flexible, and you want to keep his wind right. You don't want the dog to be under fit, but you must keep the final in mind, and build up towards it.

"The exercise you give is largely a matter of common sense. For example, if we were competing on the Thursday and again on the Saturday, my aim is to keep the dog ticking over so he is fresh for the races ahead. In the week before, I might do very little on the Sunday and Monday, and then walk the dog for a couple of miles on the Tuesday. I wouldn't gallop the dog in the week before.

"Each dog is different. You have to judge what is right for each individual. Some dogs are a bit lazy, and you need to keep them stimulated. We would give a dog like that a good walk, where he can see squirrels and pheasants, and it will freshen him up.

"In the last few days before a big final, the trick is to keep the dog calm and relaxed, and not give him too much work. If you have got the dog fit, you don't need to do too much. It is more important to keep the dog fresh. I would maybe bath a dog a couple of days before a final so that the dog feels good in himself."

TRAP DRAWS

"I sometimes think I'm the unluckiest trainer in the country when it comes to trap draws. I had one runner who was a railer, and he got trap 4 nine times in 11 outings. The draw in the 2003 Derby was unbelievable; I had three dogs running in the same heat.

"Now there are heats from which three qualify, but sometimes only two go through. I think that, in the early stages of a competition, a trainer should have his dogs separated. In the final stages, you can't do that, but it is only fair to the owners in the early stages. If you have paid a £300 entry fee, you deserve that much.

"It would also help if the trap draws were made in public so that everyone can see that fair play is being done. If you had

Don't get Charlie started on the subject of trap draws!

Droopys Natalie: It took all Charlie's skill to decide which trap she should run from.

a railer and it was drawn in trap six, at least you would know that it was the luck of the draw.

"Sometimes it can be difficult to decide where a dog should run from – particularly when they are young and just getting used to the track. Droopys Natalie started off on the rails, and then I thought she should go wider. Bob Rowe thought she should come inside, but I still said I thought she wanted to go wide. In the Oaks final (2003) she ran from trap six, and she showed that she was better running outside.

"But, in most cases, you know where a dog should run from, and it is better for everyone concerned if he gets the right box. It stands to reason that it cuts down on trouble in the race and reduces the risk of injury."

INJURIES

Unfortunately, injuries sustained during racing are all too common, and, in a big competition, the trainer is under pressure to make a decision as to whether to withdraw the dog or not. Obviously, if the injury is serious, the question does not arise, but there are minor injuries that may or may not come right in time.

"If the dog has a minor injury, such as a sore quick, you can do something about it – particularly if you have a gap between the rounds. In some big competitions, the gap between rounds is incredibly tight. For example, in the Laurels, you have to race on Thursday and Saturday, and then again the following Thursday and Saturday. That turnaround is very sharp. I would much rather enter a competition in which there is a week between each round. That gives you a chance to work with a minor injury. If you have a Thursday-Saturday turnaround, you have no chance.

"But with most injuries, you are better off withdrawing the dog. I don't want to make a fool of myself, or the dog. There is no sense in running a greyhound that is carrying an injury. The dog cannot run at his best, and you risk making the injury worse."

OFF COLOUR

A trainer always need to be aware of the health of his dogs, but most particularly when they are going through the rounds of a big competition. An injury is relatively easy to spot, but, if a dog is off colour, it can be far harder to pinpoint. However, Charlie believes that if a dog is off colour, it cannot be ignored, as it often indicates a more serious health problem that has not yet surfaced.

"In the morning, the dogs jump off their beds, and are waiting for you at the door. If a dog stays on his bed, I tend to be suspicious. Very often, that dog will not be feeling 100 per cent.

"You get to know each dog, so you recognise normal behaviour for that individual. It is easy to tell if a happy, outgoing dog is out of sorts. The hardest dogs are those that don't show any emotion. It is very hard to work out what is going on.

"In most cases, you can use appetite as a clue. If a dog won't eat his breakfast, there is usually something wrong. If a dog doesn't look as bouncy as usual, it is worth checking his temperature. I have often found that a dog is running a temperature when he appears just a little off colour, before he actually comes down with something.

Trainer's dilemma: Charlie was put under terrible pressure when Some Picture went sick in the run-up to the Irish Derby.

"If the temperature is over 101, or under 100, I would not race him. The dog is obviously below par, and will not be able to perform to the best of his ability. You also risk making the dog worse by putting the body under the stress of racing when it is not 100 per cent.

"There are times when you come under a lot of pressure to race a dog even when you know he is not right. In my early days, I sometimes raced dogs when I shouldn't have done. The owners are desperate to see the dog run, and it is very hard to let them down.

"But now I always put the dog's welfare first, regardless of the pressure. If I am not happy with a dog, I will not run him – and that is all there is to it. I know that, in the long term, it is better for both the dog and for the owner.

"I was put under terrible pressure with Some Picture. He was on a £100,000 bonus if he added the Irish Derby to his Scottish and English Derby wins, and the owner had big money on him. He went down with sickness, and we tried to nurse him through it. I got him to the final, but the dog could not run at his best."

THE FINAL

It is impossible not to be affected by nerves on the day of a big final, but Charlie's motto is to keep everything as relaxed as possible. Stick to the routine

Weighed in: Charlie likes to keep to a routine on the day of a final.

that the dog is familiar with, and then he will have no reason to fret.

"I like everything to go smoothly so that it sets the right atmosphere. If your nerves are on edge, the dog will pick it up and will not relax.

"We try to keep everything as low key as possible, and stick with the routine the dogs are used to. A finalist will be given his breakfast, and then he will be weighed, groomed and massaged. I also take the dog's temperature. I might give a dog a walk to sharpen him up, but we would not go any great distance.

"The only change in routine is that we don't gallop any dogs on the day of a big final. We have found that the extra excitement of dogs coming in and out of the kennel is disruptive, and it can set the other dogs off barking."

According to Charlie, some dogs have a natural temperament for racing, and this is a huge bonus to the trainer.

"You want a dog who is easy-going and takes everything in his stride. Rapid Ranger had a marvellous temperament for racing. He was always the type to rest in his kennel before racing, and then come out fresh and ready to go."

Over the years, trainers have come up with a variety of different ways of preparing a dog for the Derby roar, but, according to Charlie, there is nothing you can do about it.

"Some trainers go to great lengths, playing tapes, trying to get the dogs used to the noise. We always have the radio on in the kennels – and in the run-up to a Derby we would have it on pretty loud – but I don't know whether it makes any real difference. It all depends on the temperament of the individual dog. Some are laid back and take everything in their stride. Others are far more excitable."

In the 2003 Derby final, when Charlie had three runners, it was a full team turnout for the staff. Charlie handled Larkhill Bullet, Ian Sutherland had Farloe Verdict, and Chris Ackers handled Top Savings.

Charlie's rule, that whoever starts handling a dog at the beginning of a competition sticks with that dog throughout, is based on his belief that the greyhound will benefit from consistency. But there is also a touch of superstition involved. Charlie believes that keeping everything the same throughout the course of a competition brings him good luck.

"I have to admit I am a bit superstitious. If I wear a tie at the start of a competition, and we win, I have to wear the same tie for every round.

"If we set off and we realise that something has been forgotten, we never turn back and go home. I have stopped the van when we have been nearly 10 miles from home, and I have asked one of the lads to drive out from home and bring whatever it is we have forgotten. We never turn back."

WIN OR LOSE

Charlie is passionate about winning, but he is a philosophical loser.

"I'm not a bad loser. I don't begrudge anyone who wins – I always go up and shake hands with the winning trainer – but I like to think that my dog has had every chance.

"Even if I win a big race, like the Derby,

the next day it is all water under the bridge. As far as I am concerned, that particular competition is over. I've got dogs to look after and more competitions to prepare for.

"The best news is always that a dog comes off sound. Then you can forget about the disappointment, and get on with planning for the next race."

KEEPING A DOG GOING

Charlie has a reputation for keeping top dogs going over an extended period. For example, Rapid Ranger contested three English Derbies (1999, 2000, 2001); Farloe Bonus won major competitions in four consecutive years (Milton Keynes Summer Cup 1998, William Hill Stayers Classic and Milton Keynes Summer Cup 1999, Milton Keynes Summer Cup 2000, and MDC Alvin Applause Stakes 2001), and El Ronan was competing at the top level at four-and-a-half years old.

"There are a lot of factors to weigh up. It depends on the health of the dog, how prone he is to injury, and also on the dog's temperament. Ideally, a top-class dog is calm and relaxed at home, and saves everything for the track. Farloe Bonus was a lovely dog. He was so generous – and he did like Milton Keynes.

Farloe Bonus: A winner of top-class competitions over four consecutive years.

"As a general rule, I don't like to run a dog too often, particularly if you are aiming for big competitions. I would say that racing three times a fortnight is as much as any dog can take. You also have to bear in mind how much racing a dog is going to get once a competition gets underway.

"I don't believe in over-racing dogs. I think that there are only so many races in a dog, and you cannot expect a dog to keep on performing at the top level without a break.

"It is not hard to tell when a dog is getting jaded – the signs are there before you see the performance drop off on the race track. For example, if I look at a dog and his coat has lost a bit of its sheen, I would decide that it is time to give him a rest to freshen him up."

CHAPTER TWELVE

TROUBLESHOOTING

In an ideal world, every greyhound would be an easy-going type that is relaxed in the kennel, happy to be handled, and 100 per cent genuine on the track. There are some dogs like that, and trainers always value them highly. A dog that is easy to do – and has the ability to win races – is a dream come true.

However, most trainers have a fair mixture of types in their kennels, and it is a matter of finding ways of overcoming problems so that a dog can run to the best of his ability.

As the top greyhound trainer in the UK, Charlie Lister has the opportunity to hand-pick the dogs that come into his kennel. This gives him a head start in the sense that he would not consider a dog unless he was confident it was 100 per cent genuine.

"In the days when I went round the flapping tracks, we had all sorts," said Charlie. "Now I can afford to be a bit more fussy."

However, a genuine top-class racer can still bring his fair share of problems. Some dogs are highly excitable, others are very nervous, and there are some that don't get on with other dogs. It is therefore essential that training methods and management are tailored to the individual.

BAD TRAVELLERS

"Greyhounds that will not settle when they are travelling are always bad news, but it can be a nightmare if you have an open racer that will not travel. You have always got a journey ahead of you, and a dog that is fretting can exhaust himself in no time.

"I remember Spots Of Condor (winner of the 1983 Puppy Cup at Belle Vue) was a terrible traveller. He used to stand up all the way. Then we tried travelling him with a retired dog, who was a good traveller. We put them in side by side, and when the old dog lay down, Spots Of Condor followed his example. It seemed to help him to relax. After that, we always travelled the two dogs together.

"You often find that a young dog gets hyped up, but, when he gets used to the routine of travelling, he learns to settle.

"I have never tried any remedies for bad travellers or for car sickness. It is too risky with the dogs being tested."

Dual Derby winner Rapid Ranger was very laid back in his kennel, but he was unsettled when he was travelling.

Ideally, you want a greyhound who will settle down and rest en route to the track.

"He liked to have a go at the dog in the next crate. We started putting him to travel in a Magnetopulse box, and he loved it in there. He learned to settle, and he was no problem. I can remember seeing him lying on his back, completely relaxed with all four feet in the air!"

BAD KENNELLERS

"There are some dogs who will not rest in their kennel at home. They are on and off the bed all the time, jumping up at the door, and barking at every noise. If I get a dog like that, I block off the bottom half of the door so that the dog cannot see out. This does stop the dog jumping up all the time.

"If you have an excitable dog, you also have to be careful of tail injuries. Burberry Boy (winner of the 2003 East Anglian Derby) has a tail that goes like a windmill. If his tail smashes against the wall, you end up with blood everywhere. Tails are terrible to bandage, and the more the dog wags his tail, the more chance you have of the injury recurring (see page 173).

"We have found the best way round this is to keep a collar on Burberry Boy. When we go in the kennel, we can get hold of him, and stop him leaping round his kennel.

If a greyhound is destructive in his kennel, there is no option but to muzzle him.

"You do sometimes get a dog who keeps on barking in the kennel. We generally find that happens with a new dog, and, when he gets used to the routine, he settles. That type of dog may be better off being paired with another so that he has a bit of company.

"Our dogs are pretty good on the whole. They bark first thing in the morning when we are letting them out, and in the afternoon when they get their main meal, but most of the time you don't hear much from them.

"If a dog does not settle in the track kennel, it is a big problem because a dog can be in there for a long time. You could kennel at 5.30pm and not race until 10pm. If a dog keep on barking, or gets agitated, he will take an awful lot out of himself. To be honest, I would steer clear of a dog with this problem because there is very little you can do about it.

"I find that most dogs who are noisy in the kennel are quiet the second they come out."

DESTRUCTIVE DOGS

A greyhound can be surprisingly destructive, and there are many stories of dogs ripping their kennel to shreds.

"We have had dogs that chewed the bed, and then started on any other part of the kennel they could get their teeth in. We have tried putting mustard on the wooden parts of the kennel, and that can be pretty effective. Otherwise it is a matter of keeping the dog muzzled.

"Often the dog is chewing out of boredom, and this quickly develops into a habit. It can happen if a dog is injured and is confined in the kennel."

EATING MOTIONS

"This is a habit that some kennelled dogs get into. It may be a bad habit, or it may be that the dog has some kind of mineral deficiency that he is trying to make up for.

"We keep kennels and runs as clean as possible, but if we spot a dog with this problem, we would muzzle him. Sometimes this can be enough to break the habit, and the dog will not need to be muzzled after a period of time."

SELF MUTILATION

There are cases of greyhounds who chew their pads, or lick themselves excessively when they are in kennels.

"Chewing pads can be a sign of worm infestation, so it is worth checking when the dog was last been wormed. But often it is a sign of boredom. The dog will need to be muzzled, and efforts should be made to give him a change in routine."

AGGRESSIVE DOGS

Charlie is always very careful about kennelling greyhounds together, and always sticks to male-female partners. However, there are dogs that are keen to pick a fight, even if they are kennelled on their own.

"Rapid Ranger would always growl if a dog was put in the paddock next to him. We used the Magnetopulse box when we were travelling, so that he couldn't see the other dogs around him. If he was crated next to a dog, he would keep growling and worrying.

"There was no malice in him, but he was a cocky dog who liked to say: 'This is my place – I don't want other dogs in my way'. I think you've got to respect this. You don't want to try to break a dog's spirit. As soon as Rapid Ranger was racing, he would never look at another dog. He was completely genuine."

TRAPPING

Trapping ability wins races, and although Charlie trains dogs that have already been schooled, he finds that he can still work on this area.

Sometimes a young dog is slow out of the traps, or it may be that an older dog has got into bad habits, and has started turning round in the traps.

"If a dog is not trapping well, I would start by giving him a few handslips on the gallop at home. I find that this usually helps. The dog refinds his enthusiasm for chasing, and he will be sharper coming out of a trap."

Charlie has a trap at the start of his gallop, and this can be used to accustom a dog to the traps. It can also be used for retraining.

"I had one dog who kept missing his break because he turned round in the trap. It got so bad that I decided I would have to try to sort out the problem at home.

"I boarded up the front of the trap, and just left a small gap at the bottom. I then put the dog in the trap and left him while other dogs were galloped. The dog was so anxious to see what was going on, he crouched down to see through the gap at the bottom of the trap.

"I did this every day for a week, and the

A few handslips on the gallop will help to sharpen up a greyhound who is sluggish coming out of the traps.

dog got into the habit of facing the front, and crouching down to look out. When we tried him at the track, he was fine. He never turned round in his trap again."

Over many years of watching greyhounds, Charlie has discovered that dogs trap in two different ways. There are those who trap to the lure. They crouch down in the trap, listening for the sound of the lure, and the first sight of the hare. Other greyhounds, such as Some Picture, trap to the lids. The dog has his eyes on the front of the trap, and is ready to spring as the lids come up.

"This is a big advantage in some situations, such as Derby final night. The noise of the hare cannot be heard above the roar of the crowd, but if a dog has his eye on the lids, he will not miss his break."

NON-CHASERS

The best planned mating may produce some brilliant racing dogs, but there is also a high risk that a greyhound will show no interest in chasing the artificial lure.

"You can blame it on the way the dog has been reared, or it may be due to poor schooling. But you can get two dogs from the same litter and one will chase until he drops, and another simply doesn't want to know. Most non-chasers never get as far as the track, and those that do are usually incapable of running a genuine race.

"Some dogs will do better behind an artificial lure that is noisy and that rattles as it goes round. In fact, the Swaffham hare has been criticised by some for being too quiet. But it all comes down to whether you have a greyhound that genuinely wants to chase.

"There are those that go in for live kills to waken up the chasing instinct. Personally, I don't go in for that, although I know many a trainer who has done this to sharpen up a dog. But to my way of thinking, a greyhound will be quick to tell the difference between chasing a live rabbit and killing it, and being sent after an artificial lure. As soon as a greyhound gets a taste of a live kill, you risk him going off the artificial lure.

"If I want to sharpen up a greyhound, I would take him for a walk in the wood where he can see rabbits and squirrels. That will awaken his interest, and freshen him up."

FIGHTERS

"If a dog tries to fight, he is not genuine. His mind is not on chasing the lure, and there is not much you can do to change that. Dogs get into a habit of behaving in a certain way, and they will keep on repeating the same behaviour.

"If you are lucky, you may get the odd

A genuine dog will have his eye on the lure, and will be oblivious to all other distractions.

A change in routine can help a dog who has become jaded and inconsistent.

race when the dog keeps his mind on the job and chases, but he is likely to resort to the old behaviour the next time he races.

"There are those who believe that a live kill will solve the problem. I tried it many years ago, but I don't think it works. The dog will quickly return to his old ways.

"If I have a greyhound that is not genuine, I will tell the owner and suggest the dog is tried over hurdles. There is no point carrying on if you know a dog is a fighter. It will always be in his mind. You also have to think of the welfare of the dogs he is racing against. It is not fair to put valuable dogs at risk."

NOT GOING BY

"A greyhound who likes to run in company is very frustrating. It may be that the dog is not bold enough to go by, or it may be that he has not been properly schooled.

Instead of chasing the lure, he is simply running with the other dogs. All too often, this type of greyhound will have a string of seconds on his card, and you may be lucky and get the occasional win.

"You can go back to basics with schooling, or you can give the dog a course. It is not a matter of getting a kill, it is having the opportunity to course the hare."

INCONSISTENT DOGS

Sometimes a dog goes off the boil and runs below form, or he may be inconsistent, running well, and then being disappointing.

"If a greyhound's performance is not up to scratch, I would try to find ways to freshen him up. I would take him for walks in different places. It helps if a dog can see a bit of wildlife, as it makes him alert and interested.

Spring Rose was one of the most nervous dogs that Charlie has trained but when she headed for the traps, she was totally focused.

"You can also try a change of kennel, or giving him a break from the track. If a dog goes a bit sour, you must use your imagination and try to makes things different."

RACING UNDER LIGHTS

"I have found that when a young greyhound first runs under artificial lights, he can be all over the place. Shadows are cast on the track, and it can be very confusing. However, most dogs soon get used to it.

"I would always trial a dog under lights before putting him in a night-time race, so that he has a chance to adjust to the conditions."

NERVOUS DOGS

For a nervous dog, the track on a race night can be a daunting place. In most cases, a youngster will become more confident as he gets used to the routine. But there are some dogs who remain fearful.

"You do get the odd greyhound who is a bit shy and is over-faced by the crowd and the parade. It helps if this type of a dog is handled by someone he knows well – it makes the dog feel more confident.

"Spring Rose (winner of the 1996 St. Leger and Grand Prix) was one of the most nervous dogs I have ever trained. She would spin round on her lead with her tail between her legs. She didn't want to go out on to the track. But as we made our way to the boxes, she was completely different. She became focused: she wanted to get in the traps and run.

"She didn't like strangers, so we made sure she was always handled by someone she knew, but she always remained very nervous. In spite of that, she was one of the best bitches I ever trained."

RUNNING ON

The greyhounds cross the finishing line, the hare is sprung, and the dogs are caught. But what about the dog who refuses to be caught, and keeps going for another circuit or two?

"Farloe Bonus (winner of the Milton Keynes Summer Cup 1998, 1999 and 2000) was a great one for running on. It's the last thing you want because it takes so much out of the dog. The trouble is, the dog sees it as a game, and it can very good at not being caught.

"Farloe Bonus would keep on running after the hare was tripped, with his eyes glued to the hare rail. All we could do was run across the middle to cut him off before he completed a full circuit.

"Some tracks, like Sheffield, have a curtain which is drawn across the track when the hare is tripped, and that works very well.

"Dinan Wonder (winner of the 1997 Midlands St. Leger) was a pretty nervous bitch, and it was a job to catch her. There was one time when she trialled at Nottingham, and she jumped the fence, and got into the middle. We had a hell of a job trying to catch her. The racing manager was taking bets on how long it would take us!

"We finally solved the problem by making sure she was always handled by the same kennel girl when she was on the track. Dinan Wonder learnt to trust her, and so she decided it was okay to be caught."

CHAPTER THIRTEEN

HEALTH CARE

To perform on the race track, a greyhound must be at the peak of fitness. This means he must be given the correct diet and exercise, but attention must also be paid to general health and well-being.

PREVENTATIVE HEALTH CARE

Every dog needs routine preventative health treatments, but this becomes even more important when a number of dogs are kennelled together.

When living quarters and toileting facilities are shared, the risk of infection and parasites spreading between dogs becomes far greater. In a busy open race kennel, dogs are also travelling from track to track, and new dogs will be coming into the kennels at regular intervals.

At Charlie Lister's kennel, cleanliness and hygiene are top priorities (see page 88), and a close check is kept on every greyhound to ensure that all routine treatments are up-to-date.

VACCINATIONS

All racing greyhounds must be vaccinated against canine distemper, canine hepatitis, and parvo virus. These are highly contagious diseases, and they are potentially fatal. Booster vaccinations are given on an annual basis.

CANINE DISTEMPER

Preventative vaccination means that this disease is now rarely seen. The incubation period is seven to 21 days, and the first signs are a raised temperature and loss of appetite.

The dog may develop diarrhoea and a cough, and discharges may be seen from the eyes and the nose. As the disease become full blown, the dog may suffer from fits and paralysis.

CANINE HEPATITIS

This disease causes inflammation of the liver. This is not easy to recognise, but signs may include a raised temperature, sickness, pain under the ribcage (where the liver lies), jaundice and weight loss.

PARVO VIRUS

This disease had a devastating effect on greyhound kennels in the late 1970s and early 1980s, when whole litters of puppies were wiped out. Many adult dogs died, too. The signs are persistent vomiting and diarrhoea. Thankfully, an effective vaccine was developed and now the incidence of the disease is relatively rare.

INTERNAL PARASITES

In Britain and Ireland, there are basically two types of worm that commonly affect dogs – roundworm and tapeworm.

Although these parasites are not life-threatening, it is important to keep a dog free from infestation. A dog carrying a worm burden will swiftly lose condition,

and other health problems may develop.

In other countries, such as the USA and Australia, heartworm, hookworm, whipworm and lungworm, will need to be considered.

ROUNDWORM

This type of worm most commonly affects puppies. However, adults should also be routinely wormed, as this is a parasite that can migrate to humans.

The most common type of roundworm is *toxocara canis*. It is a large, round, white worm, approximately 7-15cm (3-6in) long.

A puppy with a roundworm burden will look pot-bellied, and may suffer from sickness and diarrhoea. Adult dogs rarely show such obvious signs if they are carrying roundworms, but a loss of condition may be evident.

TAPEWORMS

The most common type of tapeworm is *dipylidium caninum*, which infects the intestine. The intermediate host is the flea or louse, so external parasite control is an important part of preventative care. A dog may show poor coat condition, and small rice-like segments may be spotted around the anus.

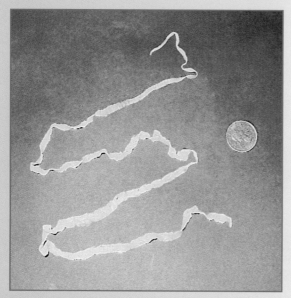

Tapeworm passed by an adult dog (the coin gives an indication of size).

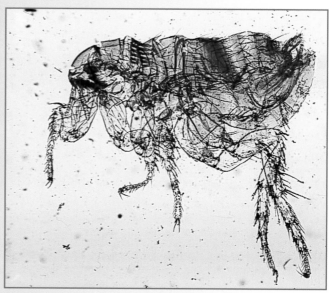

The dog flea – Ctenocephalides canis.

TREATMENT

Worming treatments are effective and easy to use. At Mudros, greyhounds are routinely wormed every six weeks.

"We worm on a regular basis so there is never a chance for a worm burden to build up. I have had dogs who have been very wormy when they arrived. It is easy to spot: the dog is generally in poor condition, with a dull coat. Often the dog is thin or struggles to put on weight."

EXTERNAL PARASITES

Routine grooming is essential, not only to keep the coat in good order, but also to keep a check for any unwelcome guests.

FLEAS

Fleas used to be a seasonal problem, but, with the advent of central heating, they have become a year-round pest.

"No matter how careful you are at home, it is inevitable that greyhounds pick up fleas. It mostly happens when they go into kennels at the track," said Charlie.

"We use a product called Duramitex. It is the same treatment that is used to spray pigeon lofts. It is a white liquid. You dilute a capful of it in water, and then you use a cloth to go over the coat. As you work through the coat, you can see if there are any fleas, or any evidence of fleas, such flea dirt.

"We groom our dogs every day, and when you use a fine-toothed comb, you can get right through the coat, and check for fleas. That means we keep on top of the situation.

"There are some greyhounds who get an allergy to flea bites, and they scratch so much that the skin gets sore. It often happens at the back of the ears. All you can do is apply some soothing cream, and make sure you keep right on top of the flea problem by checking the dogs every day. Some trainers use flea collars, but I have always found that Duramitex works well."

TICKS

These are generally picked up in areas where livestock, such as sheep and deer, graze. The tick latches on to the dog with its mouthpiece, and sucks blood until it becomes bloated.

"We used to get a lot more ticks than we do these days. I can remember one dog that was literally covered in ticks – I had never seen anything like it. It must have been so uncomfortable for the dog. Recently, it does not seem to be such a problem.

"It is important to remove the tick completely – including the mouth piece, and then we rub the dog over with Duramitex – the same treatment we use for fleas."

MANGE

This is a parasitic skin disease caused by mites. There are two types of mange: demodectic and sarcoptic.

* **Demodectic:** The small, legless parasite burrows under the skin and lives mainly in the hair follicles. Bald patches develop – usually around the face and the eyes – and it is believed that the dog's immune system is also compromised. This type of mange is spread by direct contact, but it is not as contagious as sarcoptic mange.
* **Sarcoptic:** This parasite is a surface or sub-surface feeder, and, as a result, it causes intense itchiness. The skin becomes red, inflamed and crusty, and hair loss results. This type of mange is contagious, and all in-contact animals need to be treated. It can also cause skin irritation in humans.

Charlie said: "This is a condition that we have to cope with from time to time. We use a mange skin dressing called Benzyl Benzoate, which is pretty effective.

COMMON AILMENTS

There is a wide range of ailments that can affect all dogs – and there are some that have particular relevance to racing greyhounds.

ANAL GLANDS

The anal glands are located on either side of the anus, and they are used for scent marking. If the dog cannot get rid of all the secretion in the anal sacs, they can become swollen and impacted.

"You can tell by looking if the anal glands need to be emptied – the dog may also be uncomfortable, rubbing its rear end along the ground. We use cotton wool soaked in warm water and squeeze to get rid of the contents. We would then clean up the dog using disinfectant."

BAD BREATH

Bad breath can be an indication of gum disease, but, in Charlie's kennel, teeth are cleaned on a routine basis (see page 105), so dental problems are kept under control.

However, bad breath can also indicate an accumulation of bile in the stomach, which can be detrimental to a dog's health and overall performance.

"If there is a bad smell down the throat, this usually means that there is too much

bile. I get a lump of soda and file it down so there are no rough edges. I put the soda down the dog's throat, and wash it down with a little warm milk. The dog will then vomit the bile, which is a yellow, frothy liquid. I would generally vomit a dog every couple of months. I don't like the bile to accumulate.

"Some dogs will get rid of bile naturally by eating grass and making themselves sick. But in a kennel environment, that is less likely to happen."

BALDNESS

Baldness on the back of the legs is not uncommon in greyhounds. Charlie does not see it as a great cause for concern as long as the skin is not red or sore, and the dog is not scratching.

"I have noticed that greyhounds in hard work sometimes develop baldness, and, when they have a lay off from the track, the hair grows back. I think it must be a sign of stress. There are some dogs that always keep a good coat, no matter how hard they are racing. Rapid Ranger always had a beautiful, gleaming coat. There are others that struggle to keep condition. I think nervous dogs are more prone to baldness.

"Obviously, it is important to have a

clean, deep bed, so the dog does not rub his coat. I had one greyhound that had a terrible problem with baldness, and we had a job to get the hair to grow again. We tried various creams, but you have to be so careful because a dog only has to lick his coat for the substance to show up in urine testing.

"I find the best remedy for poor coat condition is to add some suet to the diet. I either grate it and add it to the feed, or put it in the stew. It adds fat to the diet, and that does seem to help the coat."

CONSTIPATION

"If a dog is fed a well-balanced diet with plenty of fibre, constipation will not be a problem. I can honestly say that I have never had to treat a greyhound for constipation in my kennel."

COPROPHAGIA

This is the condition where a dog eats his own faeces (see page 149).

CORNS

A corn is a hard lump of pad, which can grow to cover the whole pad surface. The corn develops its own blood supply, and so it may have a very deep base set in the underlying tissues of the foot.

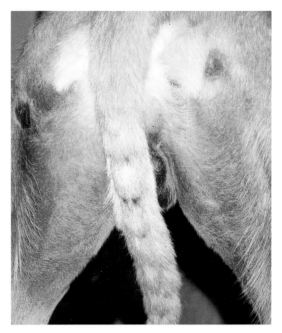

Baldness typically occurs on the thighs, and around the buttocks.

"There are various remedies for corns, but, nine times out of ten, I find they come back. I use a scalpel, and remove the centre of the corn so that it is lying below the surface of the pad, rather than being raised. This relieves the pressure, and the dog will be sound. I have found that a dog can walk lame if it is on concrete, but it can be harder to detect if the dog is on sand.

"In my experience, you can't get rid of a corn, you have to keep on cutting it back. Of course, you have to know what you are doing, or you could risk a more serious injury."

CRACKED PADS

A greyhound's pads can become hard, and, if this condition persists, cracks can develop.

"I have an old-fashioned remedy for cracked pads. I use neetsfoot oil, which my dad used for cleaning horse's tack. It is used to soften the leather in tack, and it has exactly the same effect on a dog's pad. You can use it on hard pads, and, if cracks develop, it also helps with the healing. We apply it with cotton wool, and, if necessary, we would put a sock on the foot for a couple of days to give it a chance to heal."

CRAMP

Muscle cramping can be a major problem in racing greyhounds, and a trainer needs to be aware of which greyhounds in their care have a tendency to cramp. In most cases, it affects the muscles of the loin and the back.

"Cramping affects some dogs more than others. I think it has a lot to do with fitness. It often happens when a dog has been off the track for a while and then returns to racing. When a dog comes back after a lay-off, it is important to give him some gallops, and then some trials, to get him fully fit.

"If we have a dog that has a tendency to cramp, I use a product called Tyegard. It is used for horses to prevent a condition called tying up. It contains glucose, fruit juices and citric acid, and you just add 5ml to the feed."

Charlie has also found that massage can be helpful.

"We work oil into the muscles of the shoulders and the hindquarters. It helps to get the circulation going."

He has also found that cramping can depend on the weather.

"The worst time of year for cramping is in winter. You notice it when the dog comes out of the track kennel and then hits the cold night air. All you can do is keep the dog coated, and keep him moving before the start of the race."

CUTS/BITES

In a kennel full of valuable top-class racing greyhounds, safety is a watchword. Kennels are checked daily to ensure there are no sharp edges on any of the fittings, and great care is taken if two dogs are kennelled together.

"No matter how hard you try, accidents do happen. A dog can get bitten, even though you work very hard at ensuring that dogs who are aggressive are kennelled and exercised on their own.

"If the wound is superficial, the first thing you must do is to clean it thoroughly. We use surgical spirit diluted in water, and then we would apply an antiseptic cream, such as Demisol. I also use Cut-heal. You can dab it on, or use it as a spray. If you want to keep the wound dry, a wound powder may be a better choice.

"If there is any sign of bruising, I use arnica, which I have found very effective. I also use Green Oils healing gel, which can be applied to any type of wound.

"If the wound is deep, or if it is a tear that would be difficult to heal, I would take the dog to the vet and get it stitched. You may think it doesn't look that bad, but a tear will heal much more quickly if it is stitched. The vet may prescribe antibiotics if the wound is deep."

DIARRHOEA

If a dog has loose motions, but there is no vomiting, and there is no evidence of blood in the stools, it is a relatively minor problem to deal with.

"If a dog has diarrhoea, we would not let him have his breakfast, and we would also take the bucket of water out of his kennel for a day. We would dose the dog with half

a tablet of Strinacin morning and evening, and that is usually enough to get the dog right. I would not feed meat for 24 hours.

"If there is blood in the motions, I would call the vet straightaway."

DEHYDRATION

When a greyhound is running at full stretch, particularly in hot conditions, the body can become dehydrated. The degree of dehydration can be tested with a simple pinch test. If you pinch the skin, over the neck, shoulder or flank area, it should show good elasticity and swiftly return to normal. A slow return of skin indicates dehydration. The other signs include a sunken eye, poor performance, and a slow recovery from racing. Sometimes a dog will pass small quantities of dark urine. In very severe cases, dehydration can lead to collapse.

"I have only once had a dog who was seriously dehydrated. It was a hot afternoon, and I was trialling a greyhound at Sheffield. He ran his trial, but he came off the track in great distress. His back end went and he couldn't stand up. Fortunately, we managed to get hold of a hosepipe and drenched him in cool water. He started to recover, so we took him straight to the vet. He had to be put on a

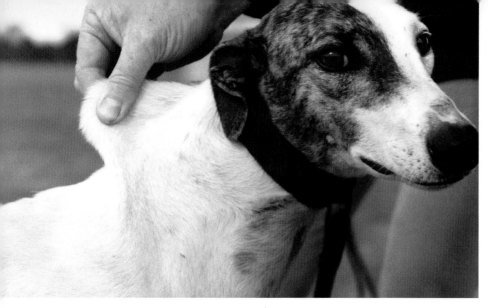

The pinch test: Pinch the skin over the neck, shoulder, or flank areas. A slow return of the skin indicates dehydration or reduced body fluid reserves.

drip, but he did make a full recovery.

"I would always get a dog checked over if he showed signs of being dehydrated because there is obviously something wrong with the dog. It may be a question of fitness if a dog is blowing a lot after a race, or there may be something else that needs to be investigated.

"Obviously, it is important to provide fresh drinking water at all times. When a dog comes off the track, we give him a drink of water with added electrolytes. This helps to replace the body salts and other minerals that are lost during the stress of racing.

"If one of my dogs has to race in hot weather, I make sure he is not put straight back in the kennel as he comes off the track. It is important to give the dog a chance to cool down properly before kennelling."
See Heatstroke.

EAR INFECTIONS

Ears need to be checked as a part of a regular grooming regime (see page 104), and they should be cleaned when necessary. If the ear is very dirty and foul-smelling, or if it appears red and inflamed, it could indicate an ear infection.

"We don't seem to get many ear problems. A greyhound's ears are erect or semi-erect, and this allows the air to circulate. It is the drop-eared dogs that get more problems," said Charlie.

"If we have a greyhound that has very mucky ears, we would use ear drops, and then give the ears a good clean, using cotton wool. We generally use Audax ear drops, but any brand will do. Sometimes a dog will keep shaking his head, and in that case, it is worth checking his ears. I once had a greyhound that got a fly in his ear. It was no problem to remove it, but it shows that it is always worth keeping a check on ears."

EYE CONDITIONS

When a greyhound is racing, it is all too easy for sand to get into the eyes. This can cause irritation, and even infection.

"As soon as a dog comes off the track, we wash the feet, and check the eyes. I find that if you literally blow the sand out of the corner of the eye – it is the best way of removing it cleanly. The next day, all the racing dogs are checked over, and we would look at the eyes to make sure there is no sign of redness or any other indication of soreness."

HEATSTROKE

Dogs can overheat very quickly, and if a dog gets heatstroke, the result can be fatal. A dog that is stressed by the heat will pant excessively as he tries to cool his body down. His body temperature will rise quickly, and this can lead to collapse, and sometimes to irreversible damage.

Greyhounds are at their most vulnerable when they are being transported in hot weather, and also if they are left out in paddocks for long periods without sufficient shade.

If a dog becomes overheated, it is imperative to lower his body temperature as quickly as possible. This can be done by hosing with cold water, or by placing ice

In hot weather, greyhounds in outside paddocks must have access to shade.

packs against the body.

Prevention is better than cure, so the best plan is to ensure that a greyhound is never left in a situation where he can become over-heated.

"When you are transporting greyhounds in hot weather, the vehicle must be properly ventilated. We have fans fitted to the roof of our vans, and if I take the car, I can use the air-conditioning.

"Our paddocks have a reasonable amount of natural shade, but, in hot weather, I would not let dogs out for long intervals. It is far better for a dog to go out four or five times a day rather than going out for a long stretch in the hottest weather. In a hot spell, we wait until later, and let the dogs out when they can appreciate the cool of the evening."

KENNEL COUGH

This is a highly infectious disease that can cause havoc in a racing kennel. The disease can spread in air-borne droplets, as well as by direct contact with other dogs. The signs are a persistent cough, which usually lasts around three weeks. Some dogs remain in relatively good health when they are infected, others may run a temperature.

"If a dog starts to cough, it is best to keep him away from the other dogs in the kennels. We have a couple of isolation kennels and runs, which we use for this purpose. It is important to get plenty of ventilation and fresh air coming into the kennel. An infected dog is only allowed access to one paddock where he is exercised on his own.

"You can do your best to keep the infection at bay by isolating an infected dog, but sometimes you are fighting a losing battle, and, in that case, I think it is better to let the disease run its course in the kennel.

"When a dog has got the cough, I dose

him with TCP, honey and glycerine. I dilute this with some warm water, and spray it down the dog's throat. I am a great believer in honey, and I find that glycerine relieves the soreness in the throat. I would use this two or three times a day. I have found that this often works better than antibiotics. I also mix a bit of butter and honey together and give it to an infected dog.

"I have found that one of the biggest problems with kennel cough is that it can linger on. A dog stops coughing and you think he has got over it, and then the cough comes back.

"When I am bringing a dog back, I would start with lead-walking exercise, and, if he isn't coughing, I would try a couple of gallops. It is only when the dog has to exert himself that you can tell whether he is clear. You don't want to rush a dog back to the track if he has had kennel cough. It is much better to wait until you are confident that he is completely over it."

Charlie has an unusual tip, which he believes keeps the kennel environment clean and healthy. He hangs strings of onions from the roof of the kennels.

"That is an old tip I got from horse racing stables. A lot of stables still do it, and I really do think it helps."

KENNEL SICKNESS

This takes the form of sickness and diarrhoea. It is a blight for a greyhound trainer, as it is highly infectious, and, once one greyhound has got it, it is likely to spread.

"We have all had to work through bouts of kennel sickness. Of course, you can help yourself to a certain extent by keeping the kennels clean and disinfected. We swill out with Jeyes fluid every day, and I think that is essential when you are keeping a lot of dogs together.

"If a dog goes down with kennel sickness, we put him in an isolation kennel. It is also important to make sure that infected dogs and healthy dogs do not relieve themselves in the same paddock.

"But no matter what precautions you take, it is very hard to stop the infection from spreading. I have had times when it has gone right through the kennel. Obviously, that means dogs cannot race. That is bad news for me, but it can be pretty devastating for a track trainer who is under contract to provide runners at every meeting.

"If a dog has kennel sickness, we give him half a tablet of Strinacin morning and evening. I take the meat out of their diet, and will probably feed half the usual amount. I don't like to starve a dog completely, but it is important that the food is fed pretty dry. I would allow the dog to drink, but I would not leave a bucket of water in the kennel. It is better to take it out, and then allow the dog a couple of chances to drink during the course of the day. In most cases, I find a dog will get over the sickness within two days.

"If a dog has gastro enteritis, and is parting with blood, I would call in the vet straightaway. This generally means the dog has to go on antibiotics, so he will probably be off racing for around 14 days.

VOMITING

Sometimes a greyhound will start vomiting but there are no accompanying symptoms, such as diarrhoea.

"When greyhounds go from track to track, it is so easy to pick up a virus. The other day I took a dog for a trial and he was perfectly well, but the next day he was vomiting.

"In this sitation, I would give no food for 24 hours – giving food just makes the problem worse. I would also dose the dog with Strinacin.

"I have to admit that I get annoyed that you can't use antibiotics to make a dog better without risking it showing up in a sample. It's not as if you are trying to enhance performance – you're just trying to make the dog better."

CHAPTER FOURTEEN

RACING INJURIES

Racing is a tough sport, and inevitably any greyhound will sustain injuries during his career on the track. Swift diagnosis is vital to ensure the dog gets the correct treatment, and then it is down to the skill of the trainer to know when a greyhound is ready to compete again.

Charlie Lister has vast experience in treating racing injuries, but he is wise enough to call in specialists when he needs them. His vet is top greyhound expert Denis Beary, who is based in Shepshed, Leicestershire. That is hardly next door to Charlie's Newark kennels, but geographical convenience is not a consideration when you are caring for the country's top greyhounds.

"I always used to go to Paddy Sweeney until he retired," said Charlie. "He was a

great man with the greyhounds. If I am really stuck he will still look at a dog for me, even though he is no longer in the game.

"You can use a local vet for routine health care, but when it comes to injuries, you really need a vet who specialises in greyhounds. I find that track vets often know nothing about greyhounds. Apart from patching up a dog, giving painkillers if necessary, it is better to wait until the next morning and go to the specialist.

"There was one time when one of my kennel lads took a dog to the track. The vet said the dog was lame, and, when the lad examined him, he found some grit in his pad and removed it. The dog was sound, but the vet insisted that he couldn't race because he had seen him walking lame.

BONE (SKELETAL) STRUCTURE OF THE GREYHOUND

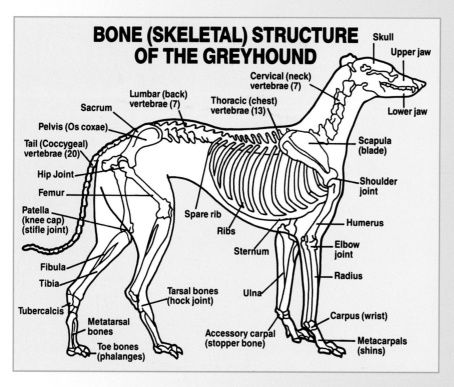

- Skull
- Upper jaw
- Cervical (neck) vertebrae (7)
- Lumbar (back) vertebrae (7)
- Thoracic (chest) vertebrae (13)
- Lower jaw
- Sacrum
- Pelvis (Os coxae)
- Scapula (blade)
- Tail (Coccygeal) vertebrae (20)
- Hip Joint
- Shoulder joint
- Femur
- Spare rib
- Patella (knee cap) (stifle joint)
- Ribs
- Humerus
- Sternum
- Elbow joint
- Fibula
- Radius
- Tibia
- Tarsal bones (hock joint)
- Ulna
- Tubercalcis
- Metatarsal bones
- Accessory carpal (stopper bone)
- Carpus (wrist)
- Toe bones (phalanges)
- Metacarpals (shins)

A trainer needs a working knowledge of a greyhound's anatomy in order to diagnose and treat injuries.

IMPORTANT MUSCLES OF THE GREYHOUND

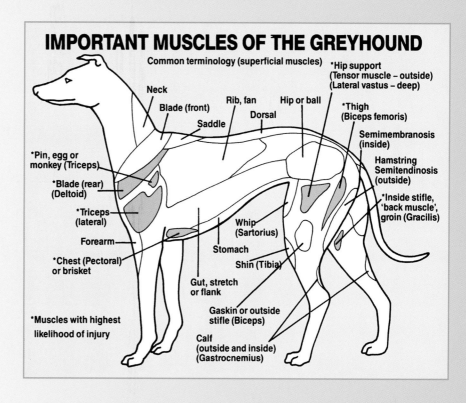

Common terminology (superficial muscles)

- Neck
- Blade (front)
- Saddle
- Rib, fan
- Dorsal
- Hip or ball
- *Hip support (Tensor muscle – outside) (Lateral vastus – deep)
- *Thigh (Biceps femoris)
- Semimembranosis (inside)
- *Pin, egg or monkey (Triceps)
- Hamstring Semitendinosis (outside)
- *Blade (rear) (Deltoid)
- *Inside stifle, 'back muscle', groin (Gracilis)
- *Triceps (lateral)
- Whip (Sartorius)
- Forearm
- Stomach
- *Chest (Pectoral) or brisket
- Shin (Tibia)
- Gut, stretch or flank
- Gaskin or outside stifle (Biceps)
- *Muscles with highest likelihood of injury
- Calf (outside and inside) (Gastrocnemius)

"They rang me up, and I said the dog was sound when he left me. I trusted the kennel lad, and if he said the dog was sound, that was good enough for me. There was a lot of argument, but, in the end, I got my way. The dog was allowed to run – and he won by five lengths!"

George Drake, a physiotherapist based in Peterborough, is the other specialist that Charlie relies upon.

"He treats all sorts of animals as well as people. He is brilliant at finding injuries, and then being able to manipulate the dog to get everything back in line. He is very successful with trapped nerves. I always examine a dog after racing, and if there is something I am unhappy about, I would take him to the physio.

"It is not hard to tell if a greyhound is injured, even if he is not obviously lame. If you examine the dog thoroughly, he will wince when you handle a sensitive area. You need to take the time and examine the dog carefully, flexing and extending the joints, and feeling over all the muscles."

THERAPIES

In Charlie's early days of greyhound racing, most of the therapies and treatments that are available today were unheard of. But Charlie is more than happy to move with the times, and he has invested in a variety of different equipment.

"The therapy machines have made a huge difference to treating injuries. In the old days we had nothing like it. All we could do was massage a dog, and then lay him off, hoping he would recover. That meant a good few dogs ended their racing careers prematurely.

"I always have a greyhound examined by the vet so that I know exactly what I am treating. I then plan a course of treatment using the therapy which seems to be the most appropriate."

MAGNETOPULSE

"I use Magnetopulse mostly for after-race soreness. I have also found it useful for hock injuries.

"You can use it on the whole dog, or you can treat a specific area. I generally use the box, and I would put a dog in for 30 minutes or so if he was sore after racing. I also find it pretty good for pulls and strains. In this case, I would give a course of treatment over several days."

ULTRASOUND

"Ultrasound is very useful for treating ripped muscles (see page 168), or for using on muscles which need building up.

You always use a gel when you are
working with ultrasound. A treatment
generally lasts four or five minutes."

PHYS-ASSIST

"This therapy is based on electrical
currents, and it has proved successful for
treating footballers and other sports
performers.

"You put gel on a drum-stick applicator,
and treat the site of the injury. The
treatment lasts for about five minutes. I
use it to treat soreness in muscles, and it
works well on the more deep-seated
muscle injuries, such as tears."

SAYRIN INTERFERENTIAL

This therapy is based on ultrasound
techniques. The foot is placed in a bucket
of water, and a dial is used to regulate the
impulses that pass through the water.

"You can test it with your hand, as it
gives a tingling sensation. You can judge
what is right for a greyhound as the dog
will flinch if the dial is too high.

"I find it very useful for treating wrist
injuries, and for building up muscle. I
would use it for about five minutes a day
over a period of a fortnight. You can tell
when a dog is improving, as it can stand
more pressure on the injury."

*Charlie generally uses the Magnetopulse
box for treating after-race soreness.*

ELECTRONIC ACUPUNCTURE

"This works on the same principle as
acupuncture. You use a pencil-like
applicator, and electric pulses pass through,
which stimulate the nerves. It is marvellous
for dealing with trapped nerves. You can
see a leg kicking when you hit a particular
nerve, and then the leg relaxes when you
have freed the nerve."

GIVING TIME

One of the greatest problems for a trainer
is deciding when an injured dog is ready to
return to the track. Charlie plays a patient
waiting game, determined to ensure the

dog is as close as possible to being 100 per cent sound before the injury is put under the stress of racing.

"I check a dog every day, and adjust the treatment if necessary. Then, when I think the dog is looking sound, I would start exercising. To begin with, this would be confined to lead walking, and then, if the dog was coping well, I would progress to the gallops. In some cases, I would try handslipping a dog halfway up the gallop to see how he went over a shorter distance.

"It is far better to wait a little longer than to rush a dog and bring it back too soon. I have learnt by my mistakes. If you race a dog when it is not sound, you risk a far more serious injury.

"The only danger with using therapy machines is that a dog can heal too quickly. If you use a machine to treat an injury, it is almost like false healing. The dog may be sound, but I sometimes worry that it has not had the deep-seated benefit of long-term natural healing. That is why I will try to give a dog a little longer than he appears to need. I continue the treatment until I can actually feel the scar tissue."

TREATMENTS

If a dog is receiving any form of treatment, he is always put in a kennel muzzle. This stops the dog worrying at the injury, and he cannot lick the cream or ointment, which would then get into his system. Charlie has learnt the hard way that you cannot be too careful when you are treating racing greyhounds.

"I had a dog called Barosa Valley, and he had to have a toe taken off his hind foot. He was off for three months and then I started to gallop him. He started to itch at the wound site, and made it sore. I went

It is essential to give a greyhound sufficient time to make a full recovery from injury.

into the chemist in Lincoln, and I got some cream that relieved itching.

"I gave it to the kennel lad, and told him to keep putting a bit on to stop the itching.

"When Barosa Valley was fit, I took him to a trial at Nottingham, and, to be honest, I had forgotten all about the cream. The flying squad (NGRC stewards who conduct random urine tests) were there, and took tests. I didn't think anymore about it. I was not at all worried about the dog. Then, three weeks later, I got a letter informing me that the test was positive.

"I was dumbfounded. I knew that dog had been given nothing illegal. I worried all night, and the next morning I asked the kennel lad to bring me the tube of cream. One of the substances in the cream was exactly the same as the one that had been named in the laboratory report. I could only assume that Barosa Valley had licked his foot, and the cream had got into his system.

"I sent all the information to the NGRC and gave a full explanation of what had happened. I even got the vet to report on the dog's medical condition, giving the history of his amputated toe. But they just chucked the whole lot out and fined me £750.

"I was so angry. The NGRC were putting their rules ahead of the welfare of a greyhound. The ridiculous thing is that if you try to ask the NGRC what you should use on a sore quick, for example, so that you will be safe with the testing, they refuse to help.

"I think the rules should be changed so at least you know what is safe to use. You cannot leave an injury such as a sore quick – it will only get worse – so what are you supposed to do? There should be someone in the NGRC who is prepared to give advice. That is the least they can do.

"You have to accept the findings of the stewards' inquiry, and you are found to be guilty even when you are not. It is very damaging to a trainer, as the public do not know the full story."

MUSCLE INJURIES

MUSCLE SORENESS
When a greyhound gallops at high speed, there will be a build-up of lactic acid in the back and hind leg muscles. This can lead to stiffness and soreness after racing.

"I find both the Magnetopulse and the Phys-Assist useful in treating this condition. You can detect soreness by working your hands over a dog, and the Phys-Assist can also help you to locate the exact spot.

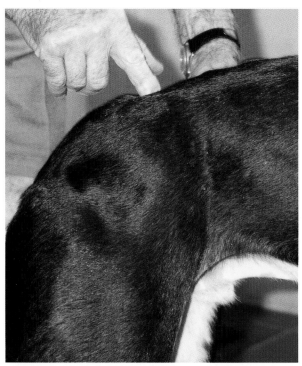

Soreness in the lower back can be checked by pressing down with the index finger between the pin bones and the spine.

"I would also work on the dog with oils. I use an American product called Trainers Choice, which I would apply on a daily basis for around a fortnight.

"If a dog is experiencing any soreness, even if it does not appear to be serious, I would leave him off the track for a couple of weeks. I don't want to risk a dog if he is not 100 per cent. If you are involved in conveyor-belt racing – supplying dogs for BAGS meetings – you can't afford to be so fussy. But I believe in giving a dog time, and taking no chances."

STRAINED/OVER-STRETCHED MUSCLES

"You can feel if a dog has a strained muscle by examining him with your hands. If you apply pressure in different places, the dog will flinch. There is no swelling, and the dog will not appear to be lame.

"Generally, this is not a big problem, and, after treatment with the Phys-Assist machine or with Ultrasound, the dog will be okay. I find the Ultrasound is good for healing. The Phy-Assist machine takes the soreness out of strains.

"In most cases, a dog would need a month off from racing. During this time, exercise would be restricted to the paddock, building up to some lead walking. Galloping would only be started when the dog was fully sound."

RIPPED/TORN MUSCLES

When a greyhound has ripped or torn a muscle, there is a hard swelling over the affected area, which will be swollen and will feel hot to the touch. The dog will walk lame.

"This injury needs Ultrasound therapy. I would probably give treatment every day for five days, then leave it for three or four days, and then give another five days' treatment.

"When you can feel the injury starting to

callus over, you can end the treatment.

"Exercise should be severely restricted, and the dog would need to be kept on a lead even when he is in the paddock.

"The time a dog is off the track would depend where the injury was, but generally I would allow six weeks. If the treatment was going well, I would start lead walking exercise in the fifth week, and, by the end of the six-week period, I would start galloping him.

"A dog can lose quite a bit of fitness after being laid off for that amount of time. I usually find the dog is ready to start trials after two or three gallops. If a dog has been off for a long time, I would start him halfway up the gallop and gradually build up fitness."

BRUISED TOE

"You usually spot this the morning after a race, when you see a toe is swollen. If there is no evidence of ligament damage, I clip back the nail, paint it with nail hardener, and then leave it. As the nail grows back, the dog will be ready for racing."

BROKEN TOE

"A dog can break his toe at any point in a race, or even when you are just giving him a gallop. It can happen on a bend, or on the straight.

"If the break is high up, with a bit of luck it should heal. But sometimes the toe will have to be amputated. A dog will return to racing, but I don't think it is quite the same.

"To an extent, it depends which toe has to be removed. The middle ones are worst, as the other toes will splay outwards, and more pressure is put on them. If an outside toe is removed, the dog will be able to keep on running, and may not be too far below his original form.

"In the old days, pin-firing was very effective. This was an operation to tighten up the ligaments around a toe joint, but you can't find anyone to do it any more. In fact, the toe was often stronger after pin-firing after it callused up."

DISLOCATED TOE

"If a toe is dislocated, the first thing I would do is cut the nail back in order to relieve the pressure. I would then put a blister on the joint. This is a strong form of iodine which you paint on the site of the injury. It hardens and that helps to tighten the joint.

"I would give the dog about four weeks off, and, by the time the nail has grown again, the dog should be ready for racing."

TOE INJURIES

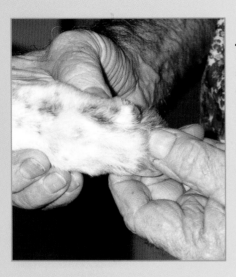

The end joint of the inside toe has been removed. A greyhound stands a better chance of recovering from this injury than if a middle toe was affected.

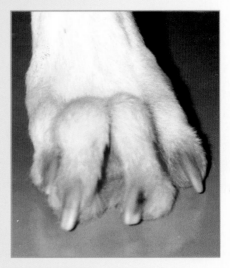

A dislocated or 'sprung toe' with swelling in the second joint.

SPLIT WEB

"If a greyhound splits his web, I would take him to the vet for treatment. The vet can cut back where the membrane has broken, and then stitch it and cauterise it. This means that the web will not split open again, which is the biggest problem with this type of injury.

"When Burberry Boy was running in the semi-finals of the Laurels, he split his web. He seemed to change legs on the back straight. He kept on running and won by seven lengths, but he came off with the injury. I could have taken a chance and run him in the final, but I decided not to risk it. If a dog is carrying an injury, he will run out of balance, and that means he could very well end up with a more serious injury."

CUT PADS

"We don't get too many cut pads as a result of racing. A dog can have hard pads, and cracks can develop, which obviously get worse under the strain of racing (see page 105).

"I have known dogs that push as they come out of the traps, and this can result in a cut on the pad.

"If you have a bad cut, there is nothing you can do, except restrict the exercise, and keep it clean. You cannot race the dog until the cut has fully healed."

TORN STOPPER PADS

A greyhound can tear his stopper pad if he is running at speed and then pulls up sharply. It is more likely to happen on hard ground.

"I use Padusol, which you apply to the affected pad. You can use it for softening the pads, and for sore quicks, but I have found it is good for healing.

"It is essential not to run the dog until the pad has healed up completely. If you run the dog too soon, the dog will catch it again. But, in my experience, they soon come right."

SAND BURNS

These can occur when the dog is going round a bend, and it is like an abrasion on the pad.

"We use Acriflex cream, and, if it is not too bad, you can keep the dog running. The secret is to be on top of the situation so that it never gets too bad. If you use a cream, they heal quite quickly.

"The worst sand burns are those between the pads, which split. They can get very deep, and then the dog cannot race.

"You sometimes get sand burns on the front feet, but they mostly affect the hind feet. It can happen in the traps if they are not kept clean. The dog is pushing from behind, and a bit of grit can cause an abrasion."

When a greyhound is travelling at speed round a bend, it is most vulnerable to sand burns.

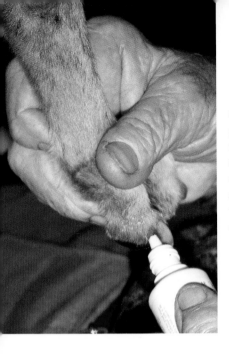

Sore quicks can generally be treated so that a greyhound can continue running through the rounds of a competition.

SORE QUICKS

Sore quicks are caused by the abrasion and collection of sand when a greyhound is galloping. Greyhounds with white nails are more likely to be affected.

"This is a problem that is most likely to occur in the winter months when the tracks are being salted.

"We always wash feet after racing, and use a small brush to go round the quicks to remove any sand. If there is a little redness or soreness, we bath the foot in methelayted spirits, and then let it dry on them. If it is bad, we apply Acriflex cream.

"In most cases, a greyhound with sore quicks can carry on racing."

SPLIT NAILS

"Routine nail clipping is essential as nails that are too long can easily be damaged.

Split nails are not uncommon when greyhounds are racing on sand.

"If the nail was just split at the end, I would file it down so that the nail was smooth and rounded. I would then apply a nail hardener. If the nail is badly split, you would not risk racing the dog."

DEWCLAWS

Dewclaws, which grow on the inside of the legs, need to be checked to ensure they do not grow inwards.

"If a dewclaw is broken, it will need to be removed. Bally Kee broke a dewclaw after running in the East Anglian Derby, but it was not much of a problem. She had to be off racing for around three weeks."

TRACK LEG

This is a condition that develops when the elbow strikes the inside of the hind leg (above the hock) as a dog is galloping. This results in bruising, and the affected area fills with fluid as blood vessels rupture under the skin.

"If I spot this injury as a greyhound comes off the track, the first thing I do is get some ice from the bar, and apply it to the site of the injury. This reduces the swelling, and stops the blood seeping under the skin. When I get the dog home,

If a greyhound deviates from its normal free-flowing galloping action, it can result in an injury such as a track leg.

I use a syringe to drain off the fluid, and then bandage it until it hardens.

"When the dog returns to racing, I use Vaseline on the elbow and on the back leg so that if they come into contact, they will glance off each other. If you react quickly, the dog can be racing again in 14 days, but it can be bad if you don't get it under control.

"I think that this injury may indicate that something is out of line. If a greyhound has a track leg, I would get him checked over properly to try to find the root cause. If you just treat the injury, you may well find that it becomes a recurring problem.

"There was one time, when I was racing at Milton Keynes, a dog came off the track, and I could see that it had a huge track leg. The trainer had no idea why the dog was losing form, even though you could see a big lump on his leg. I told them what the problem was, and, the next thing I knew that they asked me to take on the dog. We got him right and he turned out to be a good greyhound."

TAIL INJURIES

"Most tail injuries happen in the kennel, and it usually happens to the excitable dogs who never stop wagging their tails. The trouble is that once they have caught the end of the tail, it is very hard to heal, as they will keep on catching it.

"We use Friars Balsam, and then bandage the tail with cotton wool and clear tape. We try to keep the bandage as light as possible. When I am bandaging, I make sure I keep the end open so that fresh air can get in, and we can apply more Friars Balsam if necessary. The problem is that the tail is weighted at the end, and that can make it even more likely to be knocked.

"In bad cases, I get some insulation tubing, cut it down its length, and fit it to the whole length of the tail. In this way, the tail has to be held down and the dog cannot swish it around."

BROKEN HOCKS

"I have seen dogs break their hocks on bends and on straights. I have even seen it happen when a dog has not been interfered with – the joint has just come under too much pressure.

"A broken hock used to signal the end of a dog's racing career. Fortunately, that is not always the case now, but it does depend on how bad the break is. Sometimes the dog can appear to recover, but then arthritis will develop in the joint. This could show up within six months of the original injury.

"After breaking a hock, the dog would

Trouble in a race can lead to injury, but sometimes a joint simply comes under too much pressure.

be in plaster for the first three to four weeks, and exercise would be ruled out. When the plaster comes off, you need to take the dog to the paddock on a lead, and then gradually reintroduce lead-walking exercise. When a dog is recovering from this injury, you really do need to give virtually one-to-one attention. I would expect a dog to be off the track for at least three months.

"Some dogs are so brave that they can come back from a serious injury and almost shrug it off. But you can get a more faint-hearted dog who won't want to know.

"In my experience, the dog is never quite the same again. He is often slower, and you may have to limit the amount he races, perhaps only running him once a fortnight. In some cases, you have to look at the dog and decide if it would be better if he retired. If a dog is young, I reckon he's got time on his side, and it is worth persevering. But with an older dog, I wouldn't reckon it was worth it. You're not going to get enough racing out of the dog to attempt a comeback."

WRIST INJURIES

"These are the worst racing injuries of the lot. A dog can come back to race, but he will never be as good.

"Obviously, much depends on the extent of the injury, but unfortunately, wrists are notoriously difficult to heal. The greyhound can appear to be sound, but then, as soon as you start racing, the injury recurs.

"A sprain is probably the easiest wrist injury to deal with, but even then a dog will need to be off for about eight weeks. I would use ultrasound treatment to treat a sprain. I have found the Sayrin Interferential is probably the most effective form of treatment.

"If the problem is more severe, I would take the dog to the vet for an X-ray. There are a lot of bones in the wrist, and unless you have an X-ray, you don't know what the real problem is.

"There are forms of treatment, but if a dog gets a bad wrist injury, you have to accept that he will never race again at the top level."

CHAPTER FIFTEEN

SIGNING OFF

Despite a lifetime in greyhounds, Charlie Lister's passion for watching his dogs run – and win – is undiminished.

"I love going racing as much as when I first started. That's what keeps me going. I have won most of the big races, but I still want to win as much as ever. I don't like getting beat – I never have. I have always wanted to win at everything. I started with nothing, and I have worked for everything that I have achieved.

"I have also been lucky to have had some outstanding dogs in my kennel. The best dogs I have ever trained are Spring Rose, Some Picture, Rapid Ranger and Farloe Verdict, and I honestly couldn't choose between them. They were all brilliant dogs, and they were 100 per cent genuine.

"There are some races I have never won: I have been runner-up in the Oaks three times, so I have been a bit jinxed in that race. I have never competed for the Gold Collar at Romford, but I don't feel that I need to say that I have won all the classics, or anything like that. If I have a dog that suits the track and the distance, I will run him.

"Of course, I always have the English Derby in my sights – that is always the goal every year. I still get just as excited when young dogs come into the kennel. I love watching them run and seeing what distance will suit them, and where they should run from. That gives me a great thrill.

"After a big win like the Derby, people always say: 'You must have been

There will be a time when Charlie hands over – but he will always remain deeply involved in the sport he loves.

celebrating for a fortnight', but I'm not like that. I'm not the type that gets carried away. I don't need to go mad because I've won a big race. The next day, and the next race, is more important. I suppose I don't show what I feel to the outside world – but it's all going on inside my head. In my head, I *do* get carried away.

"I can't see a time when I would ever give up greyhound racing, but I can see a time when I hand over to my assistant Chris Ackers. I will take out a kennel hand's licence so that I will be involved, and I can still take dogs to the track.

"I can never imagine a week going by and not going racing…"

ROLL OF HONOUR

ALANNAS SPARK

w f b (Summerhill Gift – Persian Spark)
- **WAFCOL MIDLAND OAKS 1999**
  Track: Hall Green
  Distance: 480m
  Trap: 4
  Starting price: 3-1
  Winning time: 29.22
  Winning distance: ¾ length

ARTIE JOE

(I'm Slippy – Warm Jenny)
- **EAST ANGLIAN DERBY 1990**
  Track: Yarmouth
  Distance: 462m
  Starting price: 3-1
  Winning time: 28.57
- **MOAKES SPRINT 1991**

BALLYARD RECRUIT

bd d (Deenside Park – Bower Sinead)
- **RACING POST PUPPY CUP 1997**
  Track: Romford
  Distance: 400m
  Winning time: 24.19
  Winning distance: 1½ lengths

BANK TUNNEL

(Dads Bank – Tunnel Man)
- **NORTHERN SPRINT 1992**
  Track: Sheffield
  Distance: 290m

BELL LEGEND

bk d (Droopys Vieri – Kylies Sonia)
- **COORS BREWERY PUPPY SILVER COLLAR 2004**
  Track: Sheffield
  Distance: 500m
  Trap: 2
  Starting price: 2-1f
  Winning time: 29.32
  Winning distance: 5¼ lengths

BLEAKHILL WONDER

- **DERBY PLATE 1987**

BOWER AGNES

w bk b (Droopys Kewell – Tina At Last)
- **COLIN HARVEY NORTHERN OAKS 2003**
  Track: Belle Vue
  Distance: 465m
  Trap: 6
  Starting price: 4-1

Winning time: 27.77
Winning distance: 1¼ lengths

BRANIGANS GIG

(Justright Kyle – Castelyons Link)
• **NORTHERN FLAT 1997**
Track: Belle Vue
Distance: 460m
Winning time: 28.00

BURBERRY BOY

bk d (Top Honcho – Faultless Quest)
• **EAST ANGLIAN DERBY 2003**
Track: Yarmouth
Distance: 462m
Trap: 4
Starting price: evens f
Winning time: 28.01
Winning distance: 3¼ lengths

CALLAHOW DALY

f d (Daleys Gold – Ahaveen Fever)
• **MILLIGANS BAKERY CHALLENGE 1992**
Track: Sunderland
Distance: 450m
• **HARRY HOLMES MEMORIAL 1993**
Track: Sheffield
Distance: 500m
• **COLDSEAL PUPPY CLASSIC 1994**
Track: Nottingham
Distance: 500m

CALL ME BABY

bk b (Popov – Masonbrook Annie)
• **WAFCOL MIDLAND OAKS 2001**
Track: Hall Green
Distance: 480m
Trap: 4
Starting price: 12-1
Winning time: 28.54
Winning distance: Head

CHADWELL CHARMER

bk d (Fly Cruiser – Slippery Moth)
• **HEINEKEN PUPPY TROPHY 1994**

Track: Sunderland
Distance: 450m
• **HEINEKEN PUPPY TROPHY 1994**
Track: Brough Park
Distance: 480m

CLEAR RUN

f d (Toms The Best – Ferry Park Doll)
• **STAN JAMES ANNIVERSARY 509 2003**
Track: Swindon
Distance: 509m
Trap: 1
Starting price: 7-2
Winning time: 30.36
Winning distance: 1½ lengths

COLWINS GLORY

f d (Colwin – Riverstick Maid)
• **JOSEPH W BURLEY SPRING CUP 1999**
Grade: Open
Track: Sheffield
Distance: 500m
Trap: 5
Starting price: 5-2
Winning time: 29.67
Winning distance: 2¼ lengths

CRY HAVOC

bk d (Toe To Hand – Blink Bonny)
• **LADBROKE SPORTING SPREAD SPRINT 1997**
Track: Monmore
Distance: 210m
Winning time: 12.64

DANS SPORT

bk d (New Level – Any Band)
• **GRAND PRIX 1998**
Track: Walthamstow
Distance: 640m
Trap: 6
Starting price: 6-1
Winning time: 39.79
Winning distance: ¾ length
• **RACING POST FESTIVAL STAYERS STAKES 1998**

Track: Walthamstow
Distance: 640m

DERBAY FLYER

f d (Ayr Flyer – Brown Missile)
- **BIRMINGHAM CUP 1999**
  Track: Perry Barr
  Distance: 480m
  Trap: 1
  Starting price: 4-6f
  Winning time: 29.06
  Winning distance: ¼ length
- **WILLIAM HILL LAURELS 1999**
  Track: Belle Vue
  Distance: 465m
  Trap: 2
  Starting price: 10-11F
  Winning time: 27.80
  Winning distance: Head
- **ALL ENGLAND CUP 1999**
  Grade: Group 2
  Track: Brough Park
  Distance: 480m
  Trap: 1
  Starting price: 4-6f
  Winning time: 28.79
  Winning distance: 4½ lengths

DINAN WONDER

bk b (Druids Johno – Cavecourt Bet)
- **MIDLAND ST. LEGER 1995**
  Track: Monmore
  Distance: 647m

DRAGON KNIGHT

wbd d (New Level – Santa Rita)
- **ELLEN KILLEN STANDARD 1997**
  Track: Monmore
  Distance: 460m

DRAGON PRINCE

wbk d (Whisper Wishes – Supreme Miss)
- **WAFCOL EAST ANGLIAN CHALLENGE 1995**
  Track: Yarmouth
  Distance: 462m
- **EAST ANGLIAN DERBY 1995**

Track: Yarmouth
Distance: 462m
Starting price: 11-4
Winning time: 28.56

DROOPYS PROWLER

bk w d (Droopys Merson – Lisnakill Vicki)
- **RACING POST PUPPY STAKES 2001**
  Track: Walthamstow
  Distance: 475m
  Trap: 6
  Starting price: 9-4
  Winning time: 28.76
  Winning distance: 1¼ lengths
- **CHRISTMAS PUPPY CRACKER 2001**
  Grade: Feature
  Track: Monmore
  Distance: 480m
  Trap: 4
  Starting price: 2-1f
  Winning time: 28.36
  Winning distance: 2¾ lengths

DROOPYS SLAVE

bd d (Manorville Major – Twilight Slave)
- **PAT WHELAN MANCHESTER PUPPY CUP 1992**
  Track: Belle Vue
  Distance: 460m
- **NORTHUMBERLAND GOLD CUP 1993**
  Track: Brough Park
  Distance: 480m
- **NORTHUMBERLAND GOLD CUP 1994**
  Track: Brough Park
  Distance: 480m

DRUMSNA POWER

bd b (Asbury Park – Drumsna Beauty)
- **STAYERS GRAND 1998**
  Track: Belle Vue
  Distance: 645m
  Trap: 1
  Starting price: 3-1
  Winning time: 40.58
  Winning distance: 2¼ lengths

EGMONT JOAN

f b (Daleys Gold – Egmont Biddy)
- **NORTHERN OAKS 1995**
  Track: Belle Vue
  Distance: 460m

EL RONAN

bd d (Staplers Jo – Freds Flame)
- **WILLIAM HILL GOLD CUP 2001**
  Track: Oxford
  Distance: 450m
  Trap: 1
  Starting price: 4-6f
  Winning time: 27.10
  Winning distance: ½ length
- **WAFCOL EAST ANGLIAN CHALLENGE 2001**
  Track: Yarmouth
  Distance: 462m
  Trap: 2
  Starting price: 2-1
  Winning time: 28.25
  Winning distance: 2¾ lengths
- **REGAL GOLD CUP 2002**
  Track: Sunderland
  Distance: 450m
  Trap: 4
  Starting price: 9-4 f
  Winning time: 27.47
  Winning distance: 4 lengths
- **MILTON KEYNES DERBY 2002**
  Track: Milton Keynes
  Distance: 440m
  Trap: 5
  Starting price: 5-2f
  Winning time: 26.68
  Winning distance: 1 length

ENDON TIGER

bd d (Slaneyside Hare – Kevalnig Kate)
- **ALL ENGLAND CUP 1997**
  Track: Brough Park
  Distance: 480m
  Trap: 6
  Starting price: 4-6f
  Winning time: 29.10

FARLOE BONUS

w bd d (Alpine Minister – Farloe Post)
- **MILTON KEYNES SUMMER CUP 1998**
  Grade: Feature
  Track: Milton Keynes
  Distance: 620m
  Starting price: 4-1
  Winning time: 37.86 (Track record equiv.)
  Winning distance: 6¼ lengths
- **WILLIAM HILL STAYERS CLASSIC 1998**
  Grade: Open
  Track: Sheffield
  Distance: 660m
  Trap: 2
  Starting price: 10-11f
  Winning time: 39.67
  Winning distance: 2 lengths
- **MILTON KEYNES SUMMER CUP 1999**
  Track: Milton Keynes
  Distance: 620m
  Trap: 3
  Starting price: 1-3f
  Winning time: 37.98
  Winning distance: 2¼ lengths
- **MILTON KEYNES SUMMER CUP 2000**
  Track: Milton Keynes
  Distance: 620m
  Trap: 2
  Starting price: 6-4f
  Winning time: 38.00
  Winning distance: 7 lengths
- **MDC ALVIN PR APPLAUSE STAKES 2001**
  Track: Hove
  Distance: 695m
  Trap: 1
  Starting price: 11-4
  Winning time: 41.85
  Winning distance: 3¾ lengths

FARLOE BRAZIL

f d (Mr Bozz – Farloe Dingle)
- **JOHN SMITHS BREEDERS PUPPY CUP 2003**
  Track: Nottingham
  Distance: 500m
  Trap: 1
  Starting price: 11-4
  Winning time: 30.12
  Winning distance: 2¾ lengths

- **LADBROKES GOLD CUP 2003**
  Track: Monmore
  Distance: 480m
  Trap: 4
  Starting price: 9-2
  Winning time: 28.12
  Winning distance: 2½ lengths

FARLOE FORTY

bk d (Top Honcho – Free Chance)
- **REGAL PUPPY TROPHY 2002**
  Track: Sunderland
  Distance: 450m
  Trap: 1
  Starting price: 7-4
  Winning time: 27.74
  Winning distance: 6¼ lengths

FARLOE TOTTY

bk w b (Plasterscene Gem – Listen To Reason)
- **PETERBOROUGH PUPPY CESAREWITCH 2001**
  Track: Peterborough
  Distance: 605m
  Trap: 1
  Starting price: 11-2
  Winning time: 37.95
  Winning distance: 1¼ lengths

FARLOE VERDICT

bk b (Droopys Vieri – She Knew)
- **WILLIAM HILL BLUE RIBAND 2003**
  Track: Hall Green
  Distance: 480m
  Trap: 1
  Starting price: 5-2
  Winning time: 28.09 (T.R.)
  Winning distance: 2 lengths
- **WILLIAM HILL GREYHOUND DERBY 2003**
  Track: Wimbledon
  Distance: 480m
  Trap: 2
  Starting price: 12-1
  Awarded the race following the disqualification of Droopys Hewitt
- **TOTETSPORT SCOTTISH DERBY 2004**
  Track: Shawfield

Distance: 480m
Trap: 2
Starting Price: 11-4
Winning time: 28.79 (T.R.)
Winning distance: 5¼ lengths

FOXCOVER LIZZIE

w bk b (I'm His – Forever Susan)
- **REGAL STAYERS TROPHY 1999**
  Track: Shawfield
  Distance: 670m
  Trap: 3
  Starting price: 5-2
  Winning time: 41.33
  Winning distance: 9 lengths

FOX FIRE

- **MACWORTH DASH 1981**
  Track: Derby
  Distance: 246m

GAYTIME DEAN

f d (Deenside Joker – Gaytime Steffi)
- **CHRISTMAS CRACKER 1998**
  Track: Milton Keynes
  Distance: 440m

GLAMOUR HOBO

f d (Nameless Star – Glamour Show)
- **THE SILK CUT 480 1995**
  Track: Gosforth
  Distance: 480m
- **BEDFORDSHIRE DERBY 1995**
  Track: Henlow
  Distance: 484m
  Winning time: 29.20
  Starting price: 7-4f
- **STRONGBOW CUP 1996**

GULLEN SLANEY

bd w d (Slaneyside Hare – Gulleen Elsa)
- **PETER DERRICK NATIONAL SPRINT CHAMPIONSHIP 1999**
  Track: Nottingham
  Distance: 300m

Trap: 6
Winning time: 18.07
Winning distance: 1½ lengths

HARRYS BOY BLUE

be d (Tico – Soviet Supreme)
• **DEAN JACKSON MEMORIAL TROPHY 1995**
Track: Hull
Distance: 490m

JERS PICK

• **PEPSI COLA SPRINT 1987**
Track: Yarmouth
Distance: 277m

JUST RIGHT KYLE

(Kyle Jack – I'm A Duchess)
• **McLAREN INVITATION 1993**
• **ARCHIE SCOTT MEMORIAL TROPHY 1993**
Track: Hall Green
Distance: 474m
• **EAST ANGLIAN DERBY 1993**
Track: Yarmouth
Distance: 462m
Winning time: 28.30
• **MIDLAND FLAT CHAMPIONSHIP 1993**
Track: Hall Green
Distance: 474m
Starting price: 3-1
Winning time: 29.04
• **GORTON CUP 1994**
Track: Belle Vue
Distance: 460m

KILLEENAGH DREAM

wbd d (Dads Bank – Killeenagh Lady)
• **KEY 1993**
Track: Wimbledon
Distance: 868m
• **CESAREWITCH 1993**
Track: Belle Vue
Distance: 855m
Starting price: 20-1
Winning time: 55.21
• **WILLIAM HILL INVITATION 1993**

KING OSCAR

wbd d (Polnoon Chief – Keston Queen)
• **CAFFREYS NEW TRACK TROPHY 1997**
Track: Monmore
Distance: 264m
• **QUICKSILVER STAKES 1997**
Track: Romford
Distance: 400m
• **GOLDEN SPRINT 1997**
Track: Romford
Distance: 400m
Starting price: 4-5f
Winning time: 24.33

KIT KAT KID

bk d (Some Picture – With A Vengance)
• **COLDSEAL PUPPY CLASSIC 1999**
Track: Nottingham
Distance: 500m
Trap: 6
Starting price: 10-11f
Winning time: 30.56
Winning distance: ¾ length
• **HARDYS JUVENILE INVITATION 1999**
Track: Sheffield
Distance: 500m

KNOCKAUN JOKER

f d (Deenside Joker – Gaytime Steffi)
• **DRANSFIELD STAYERS 2002**
Track: Belle Vue
Distance: 647m
Trap: 1
Starting price: 4/6f
Winning time: 39.87
Winning distance: 3¾ lengths
• **DERBY PURSE 2002**
Track: Yarmouth
Distance: 659m
Trap: 4
Starting price: 4-5f
Winning time: 41.05
Winning distance: 3¾ lengths

KNOCKTOOSH QUEEN

bk b (Torbal Piper – Knocktoosh Fancy)
- NIGEL TROTH YORKSHIRE OAKS 2003
  Track: Sheffield
  Distance: 500m
  Trap: 2
  Starting price: 11-4
  Winning time: 29.53
  Winning distance: 1¾ lengths
- FOSTERS NATIONAL OAKS TROPHY 2003
  Track: Nottingham
  Distance: 480m
  Trap: 3
  Starting price: 11-10f
  Winning time: 28.63
  Winning distance: 2¼ lengths
- BOOKMAKERS CATEGORY TWO STAKES 2003
  Track: Sheffield
  Distance: 500m
  Trap: 2
  Starting price: Evensf
  Winning time: 29.80
  Winning distance: 3¼ lengths

LARKHILL BULLET

bd d (Staplers Jo – Annies Bullet)
- JP CONSTRUCTION NORTHERN SPRINT 2002
  Track: Sheffield
  Distance: 280m
  Trap: 6
  Starting price: 8-11f
  Winning time: 16.51
  Winning distance: 2 lengths
- EAST ANGLIAN DERBY 2002
  Track: Yarmouth
  Distance: 462m
  Trap: 6
  Starting price: 6-4f
  Winning time: 28.22
  Winning distance: 3½ lengths

LISSENAIR LUKE

f d (Ardfert Dan-Suir Dew)
- WILLIAM HILL GOLD SCURRY CUP 1999
  Track: Catford

Distance: 385m
Trap: 4
Starting price: 3-1jf
Winning time: 23.49
Winning distance: 4¾ lengths

LYONS TURBO

(Evelyn Turbo – Miss Time Up)
- STEEL CITY CUP 1988
  Track: Sheffield
  Distance: 500m
  Starting price: 5-6f
  Winning time: 30.29

MEANUS DUKE

- MANCHESTER PUPPY CUP 1979
  Track: Belle Vue
  Distance: 460m

MICKS MYSTIC

bk d (Come On Ranger – Tracys Lady)
- REGAL SCOTTISH DERBY 2003
  Track: Shawfield
  Distance: 480m
  Trap: 5
  Starting price: 4-6f
  Winning time: 29.07
  Winning distance: 5 lengths

MONARD WISH

bd b (Whisper Wishes – Solas An Maiden)
- COCK O' THE NORTH 1993
  Track: Belle Vue
  Distance: 645m
- WALTHAMSTOW BOOKMAKERS INVITATION 1994
  Track: Walthamstow
  Distance: 640m

MOYNIES CASH

bd d (Joannestown Cash – Glanamoon)
- STAN JAMES GYMCRACK PUPPY CHAMPIONSHIP 2003
  Track: Hall Green
  Distance: 480m

Trap: 6
Starting price: 13-2
Winning time: 28.45
Winning distance: ½ length

NIGHT RUNNER

wbd d (Knockrour Slave – Hi There Linda)
• **NORTHERN SPRINT CHAMPIONSHIP 1986**
Track: Sheffield
Distance: 290m
Starting price: 11-8f
Winning time: 16.94

PARLIAMENT ACT

bd d (Trade Official – Lemon Ashling)
• **JP CONSTRUCTION NORTHERN SPRINT 2000**
Track: Sheffield
Distance: 280m
Trap: 4
Starting price: 6-1
Winning time: 16.38
Winning distance: 2½ lengths
• **PEPSI COLA SPRINT 2001**
Grade: Open
Track: Yarmouth
Distance: 277m
Trap: 1
Starting price: 2-5f
Winning time: 16.71
Winning distance: 1½ lengths

RAPID RANGER

bd d (Come On Ranger – Rapid Vienna)
• **DRANSFIELD LOTTERIES PUPPY CUP 1999**
Track: Sheffield
Distance: 500m
• **WILLIAM HILL GREYHOUND 2000**
Track: Wimbledon
Distance: 480m
Trap: 2
Starting price: 7-4f
Winning time: 28.71
Winning distance: 3½ lengths
• **WILLIAM HILL GREYHOUND DERBY 2001**
Track: Wimbledon
Distance: 480m
Trap: 4

Starting price: 7-4
Winning time: 28.71
Winning distance: $3^1/4$ lengths

RATHER SPECIAL

bk d (Snowflash – K's Expression)
• **BAGS GUINEAS 1998**
Track: Swindon
Distance: 480m
Trap: 6
Starting price: 9-4
Winning time: 29.12
Winning distance: ½ length

RISK IT MISS

wbk b (The Other Risk – Wish Miss)
• **DIAMOND JUBILEE 500 1991**
Track: Sheffield
Distance: 500m
• **MILLIGANS BAKERY CHALLENGE 1992**
Track: Sunderland
Distance: 450m

SESKIN ROBERT

bk d (Spiral Nikita – Seskin Claire)
• **LADBROKES FESTIVAL 480 2002**
Track: Monmore
Distance: 480m
Trap: 5
Starting price: 7-2
Winning time: 28.79
Winning distance: ½ length

SEXY DELIGHT

bk b (Some Picture – Spring Rose)
• **EVENING STANDARD TV TROPHY 2000**
Track: Wimbledon
Distance: 868m
Trap: 1
Starting price: 9-4f
Winning time: 54.51
Winning distance: Head
• **TEAMTALK.COM TROPHY 2001**
Track: Hove
Distance: 695m
Trap: 1

Starting price: 11-4
Winning time: 41.49
Winning distance: 4¾ lengths
• **STOW MARATHON 2001**
    Track: Walthamstow
    Distance: 840m
    Trap: 1
    Starting price: 1-2f
    Winning time: 53.36
    Winning distance: 3¾ lengths

SIMPLY FREE

bk b (Daleys Gold – Rooskey Critic)
• **MIDLAND OAKS 1993**
    Track: Hall Green
    Distance: 474m
• **YORKSHIRE OAKS 1993**
    Track: Sheffield
    Distance: 500m
• **SELECT STAKES 1993**
    Track: Wembley
    Distance: 490m
    Starting price: 7-1
    Winning time: 29.16
• **BOXING DAY MATCH 1993**

SLIDEAWAY SNOOPY

(Michigan Man – Marys Mascot)
• **SUNDERLAND OAKS 1990**
    Track: Sunderland
    Distance: 450m
• **PETERBOROUGH CESAREWITCH 1990**
    Track: Peterborough
    Distance: 605m
    Starting price: 7-2
    Winning time: 38.11
• **THOUSAND POUNDER 1990**

SOME PICTURE

bk d (Slaneyside Hare – Spring Season)
• **PETER DERRICK ECLIPSE 1996**
    Track: Nottingham
    Distance: 500m
    Starting price: 3-1jf
    Winning time: 29.83
• **TONY MORRIS SELECT STAKES 1996**
    Track: Wembley

Distance: 490m
Starting price: 9-4f
Winning time: 28.91
• **KNOW SOMETHING STAKES 1997**
    Track: Nottingham
    Distance: 500m
• **REGAL SCOTTISH DERBY 1997**
    Track: Shawfield
    Distance: 480m
    Trap: 5
    Starting price: evensf
    Winning time: 29.20
    Winning distance: 2 lengths
• **DAILY MIRROR/SPORTING LIFE GREYHOUND DERBY 1997**
    Track: Wimbledon
    Distance: 480m
    Trap: 6
    Starting price: 8-13f
    Winning time: 28.23
    Winning distance: 6¼ lengths

SOVIET KING

bk d (Come On Ranger – Soviet War)
• **LADBROKES FREEPHONE SPRINT TROPHY 2002**
    Track: Nottingham
    Distance: 300m
    Trap: 6
    Starting price: 4-6f
    Winning time: 17.90
    Winning distance: 1¼ lengths

SPENWOOD MAGIC

(Westmead Claim – Loopy Lill)
• **WILLIAM KING CUP 1993**
    Track: Shawfield
    Distance: 670m
• **REGAL STAYERS 1993**
• **DRANSFIELD ST. LEGER 1993**
    Track: Sheffield
    Distance: 730m

SPOTS OF CONDOR

bd d (Lindas Champion – Spots of Sanyo)
• **TETLEY/SKOL MANCHESTER PUPPY CUP 1983**

Track: Belle Vue
Distance: 460m

SPRING ROSE

w f b (Galtymore Lad – Rachels Baby)
- **GRAND PRIX 1996**
  Track: Walthamstow
  Distance: 640m
  Winning time: 39.05
  Winning distance: 8 lengths
- **WENDY FAIR ST. LEGER 1996**
  Track: Wembley
  Distance: 655m
  Winning time: 39.29 (T.R.)
  Winning distance: 7½ lengths

STOUKE SLIPPY

w bk d (Murlens Slippy – Stouke Pet)
- **RAPID RACELINE INVITATION 1995**
  Track: Belle Vue
  Distance: 460m

SUNCREST SAIL

bebdw d (Low Sail – Sarahs Surprise)
- **NGRC STEWARDS CUP 1995**
  Track: Walthamstow
  Distance: 640m
- **REGENCY 1995**
  Track: Hove
  Distance: 740m
  Starting price: 1-20f
  Winning time: 44.26
- **DRANSFIELD NOVELTY EBOR 1995**
  Track: Sheffield
  Distance: 660m
- **GRAND PRIX 1995**
  Track: Walthamstow
  Distance: 640m
  Starting price: 11-10f
  Winning time: 39.62
- **REGAL ST LEGER 1995**
  Track: Shawfield
  Distance: 670m
- **BBC TV TROPHY 1996**
  Grade: Group 2
  Track: Walthamstow
  Distance: 840m

Starting price: 7-2
Winning time: 51.75
- **DRANSFIELD EBOR 1996**
  Track: Sheffield
  Distance: 660m
- **WILLIAM KING CUP 1996**
  Track: Shawfield
  Distance: 670m

SUNHILL MISTY

bd b (Kyle Jack – Game Misty)
- **PEPSI COLA MARATHON 1994**
  Track: Walthamstow
  Distance: 820m
  Winning time: 53.10
- **DAILY RECORD MARATHON 1994**
  Track: Shawfield
  Distance: 932m

SUPERIOR CHAMP

- **SILVER SALVER 1978**
- **NORTHERN SPRINT CHAMPIONSHIP 1980**
  Track: Sheffield
  Distance: 290m

SURE FANTASY

(Phantom Flash – Lively Sparkii)
- **PETERBOROUGH PUPPY DERBY 1993**
  Track: Peterborough
  Distance: 420m
  Winning time: 25.83
- **NOVEMBER GRAND 1993**
  Track: Sheffield
  Distance: 500m
- **XMAS CUP 1993**
  Track: Sheffield
  Distance: 500m
- **ARCHIE SCOTT BENEVOLENT TROPHY 1994**
  Track: Hall Green
  Distance: 474

SWIFT BAND

f d (Yellow Band – Swift Lass)
- **EAST ANGLIAN DERBY 1981**
  Track: Yarmouth
  Distance: 462m

Starting price: 7-4
Winning time: 28.33

TAILORS NOEL

bk d (Balinderry Ash – Tailors Rush)
• **NORTHERN SPRINT 1995**
  Track: Sheffield
  Distance: 290m

TAMMYS DELIGHT

(Waltham Abbey – Lulus Moth)
• **DRANSFIELD NOVELTY EBOR 1994**
  Track: Sheffield
  Distance: 660m

TERRYDRUM KATE

wf b (Amidus Slippy – Rathbeg Crystal)
• **EAST ANGLIAN DERBY 1997**
  Track: Yarmouth
  Distance: 462m
  Starting price: 11-4
  Winning time: 28.28
• **NORTHERN OAKS 1998**
  Track: Belle Vue
  Distance: 460m
  Trap: 6
  Starting price: 4-11f
  Winning time: 28.53
  Winning distance: 1¼ lengths

TOBLERMOREY BOY

f d (Spiral Nikita – Lemon Polly)
• **HARDY BOOKMAKERS CHAMPION STAKES JUVENILE 2000**
  Track: Sheffield
  Distance: 500m
  Trap: 5
  Starting price: 2-1
  Winning time: 29.82
  Winning distance: Neck
• **ALL ENGLAND CUP 2000**
  Track: Brough Park
  Grade: Group 2
  Distance: 480m
  Trap: 6
  Starting price: 1-2f

Winning time: 28.68
Winning distance: 6¼ lengths

TOMS AUTUMN

bk d (Toms The Best – Autumn Rain)
• **LADBROKE DOTCOM PUPPY TROPHY 2002**
  Track: Nottingham
  Distance: 500m
  Trap: 4
  Starting price: 7-2
  Winning time: 30.34
  Winning distance: 4¼ lengths

TOP SAVINGS

bk w d (Top Honcho – Too Breezy)
• **BOOKMAKERS GUINEAS 2003**
  Track: Nottingham
  Distance: 500m
  Trap: 5
  Starting price: 1-3f
  Winning time: 29.63
  Winning distance: 5¼ lengths

TRUE HONCHO

be w d (Top Honcho – Security Special)
• **TOMSTHEBEST.COM 2002**
  Grade: Open
  Track: Hove
  Distance: 695m
  Trap: 3
  Starting price: 5-4
  Winning time: 41.03
  Winning distance: 4¾ lengths

WESTMEAD STRIKER

w bd d (Daleys Denis – Westmead Chick)
• **GARY WILTSHIRE MIDLAND FLAT 1999**
  Track: Hall Green
  Distance: 480m
  Trap: 2
  Starting price: 5-1
  Winning time: 28.46
  Winning distance: 1 length

WISE EMERALD

bd w d (Trade Official – Try A Minnie)
- **GARY WILTSHIRE MIDLAND FLAT 2000**
  Track: Hall Green
  Distance: 480m
  Trap: 6
  Starting price: 4-1
  Winning time: 28.31
  Winning distance: 3 lengths

YELLOW COWBOY

bd d (Yellow Ese-Lenas Blackie)
- **FIRST RADIO LUXEMBOURG INVITATION STAKES 1982**
  Track: Crayford
  Distance: 462m

INDEX OF NAMES, PLACES AND SPORTING EVENTS